Taxcafe Tax Guides

Pension Magic

How to Make the Taxman Pay
for Your Retirement

By Nick Braun PhD

Important Legal Notices:

Published by:
Taxcafe UK Limited
67 Milton Road
Kirkcaldy KY1 1TL
Tel: (0044) 01592 560081
Email: team@taxcafe.co.uk

14th Edition, December 2022

ISBN 978-1-911020-77-6

Disclaimer

1. This guide is intended as **general guidance** only and does NOT constitute accountancy, tax, financial, investment or other professional advice.

2. The author and Taxcafe UK Limited make no representations or warranties with respect to the accuracy or completeness of this publication and cannot accept any responsibility or liability for any loss or risk, personal or otherwise, which may arise, directly or indirectly, from reliance on information contained in this publication.

3. Please note that tax legislation, the law and practices by Government and regulatory authorities (e.g. HM Revenue & Customs) are constantly changing. We therefore recommend that for accountancy, tax, financial, investment or other professional advice, you consult a suitably qualified accountant, tax advisor, financial adviser, or other professional adviser.

4. Please also note that your personal circumstances may vary from the general examples given in this guide and your professional adviser will be able to give specific advice based on your personal circumstances.

5. This guide covers UK taxation only and any references to 'tax' or 'taxation', unless the contrary is expressly stated, refer to UK taxation only. Please note that references to the 'UK' do not include the Channel Islands or the Isle of Man. Foreign tax implications are beyond the scope of this guide.

6. All persons described in the examples in this guide are entirely fictional. Any similarities to actual persons, living or dead, or to fictional characters created by any other author, are entirely coincidental.

Dedication

To Sandy, one of my much loved sons.

About the Author & Taxcafe

Dr Nick Braun founded Taxcafe in 1999, along with his partner Aileen Smith. As the driving force behind the company, their aim is to provide affordable plain-English tax information for private individuals, business owners and professional advisors.

Over the past 23 years Taxcafe has become one of the best-known tax publishers in the UK and has won several prestigious business awards.

Nick has been a specialist tax writer since 1989, first in South Africa, where he edited the monthly *Tax Breaks* publication, and since 1999 in the UK, where he has authored several tax books including *Small Business Tax Saving Tactics* and *Salary versus Dividends*.

Nick also has a PhD in economics from the University of Glasgow, where he was awarded the prestigious William Glen scholarship and later became a Research Fellow.

Contents

Introduction

Let's get straight down to business. There is only one reason why you should put money into a pension and that is to SAVE TAX.

As a pension saver you enjoy two important tax reliefs:

- Tax relief on your contributions – what I call buying investments at a 40% discount.

- Tax-free growth – all your income and capital gains are completely tax free.

However, if maximising tax relief is your priority, as it should be, there's a lot more to it than simply putting away a fixed amount each year.

You may wish to decide *how much* to invest, making bigger or smaller pension contributions in some years or none at all.

You may wish to consider *who* makes the contributions: you, your employer, or your spouse or partner.

You may also want to look at *when* is the best time to invest.

And, of course, you may want to know *why* you should even bother investing in a pension in the first place. For example, are pensions better than other investment vehicles such as ISAs and Lifetime ISAs?

All of these important issues are addressed in this guide and I think you will be surprised by some of the results.

In Part 1 we examine how tax relief on pension contributions is calculated and how much you are allowed to invest. However, as we shall discover, calculating the maximum pension contribution you *can* make is not as important as calculating the maximum pension contribution you *should* make to maximise your tax relief.

Over 200,000 people do not claim all the tax relief to which they are entitled, so we also examine how you can make a backdated tax relief claim and avoid other common mistakes that could cost you thousands of pounds.

Pension Freedom

Up until a few years ago the amount of money you could withdraw from your pension was tightly controlled. Most individuals' savings could only come out at a trickle, either through an annuity or something called "capped drawdown".

These restrictions have now been lifted completely, giving pension savers more control over their money than they have ever had.

Once you reach the minimum retirement age (currently 55) you have complete freedom to withdraw as much or as little money as you like from your pension pot, whenever you like.

As a result, pension savers have the ability to control their tax bills, by making big pension withdrawals in some tax years and smaller withdrawals in others.

The Government has also removed another of the major obstacles that put people off using pensions to save for retirement. Up until a few years ago, when you died your remaining pension savings were taxed at 55% before being passed on to certain family members.

This hefty tax charge has been abolished and pension pots can be inherited by family members with no adverse tax penalties.

In Part 2 of the guide we explain all of the "Pension Freedom" changes and show you how to save thousands of pounds in both income tax and capital gains tax by timing your pension withdrawals carefully.

In Part 3 we show how pensions are much more powerful tax shelters than ISAs. We track two investors over a number of years and reveal that a pension saver could end up with 41.67% more retirement income than an ISA investor.

We also explain some of the lesser known tax differences between ISAs and pensions (for example, why some dividend income is taxed inside an ISA and why your family may be better off if your money is in a pension).

Those under the age of 40 can open a "Lifetime ISA" and use it to save either for a first home or for retirement.

Part 3 tells you everything you need to know about this fantastic saving vehicle and why some taxpayers could end up with 17.6% more retirement income if they use a Lifetime ISA instead of a traditional pension.

Postponing & Accelerating Pension Contributions

In Part 4 we look at the pros and cons of postponing and accelerating pension contributions. We show how basic-rate taxpayers – those earning under £50,270 – can increase their pension pots by 33% by delaying making pension contributions for several years.

This part of the guide also contains a fascinating case study which reveals that, even if you postpone pension contributions for several years you will not necessarily end up one penny worse off than someone who makes pension contributions for many years.

There is one group who should always consider making pension contributions: households where the highest earner's income is between £50,000 and £60,000 and child benefit is being claimed. Your family's child benefit payments are steadily taken away as your income rises from £50,000 to £60,000. By using pension contributions to reduce taxable income, people in this income bracket can enjoy tax relief of up to 74% or more!

Part 4 also contains a special chapter for high income earners. We will see how those earning between £100,000 and £150,000 can enjoy between 50% and 60% tax relief on their pension contributions. This is because pension contributions reduce your 'adjusted net income' which allows you to recoup your income tax personal allowance.

This chapter also explains the special rules for the highest income earners who may only be able to make pension contributions of £4,000 per year (the so-called 'tapered annual allowance') if their income exceeds £200,000.

Employees, Business Owners & Landlords

In Parts 5 to 8 we look at different types of pension saver: salaried employees, company owners, the self employed and landlords.

In Part 5 we explain 'auto-enrolment': the compulsory pensions that have helped many employees enjoy a pension contribution from their employer for the first time. Some individuals who can receive this free money from their employers may decide to opt out. So in this section we publish an interesting table which shows just how much bigger your pension pot will be if you take full advantage of pension contributions from your employer.

Part 6 looks at salary sacrifice pensions, which can boost your pension contributions by an astonishing 34%. Salary sacrifice allows you to claw back not just income tax but *national insurance* as well, including the 13.8% paid by your employer. A salary sacrifice pension is arguably the most powerful tax-saving tool available to salaried employees.

Part 7 covers company owners and directors and reveals why company pension contributions are now, more than ever, a highly tax-efficient way to extract money from your business. We also explain why getting your company to make the contributions is more tax efficient than making the contributions yourself.

There is also a chapter looking at the benefits and drawbacks of using your pension to make a loan to your company – you can do this if you have a small self-administered pension scheme (SSAS).

Most of this guide is relevant to the self employed (sole traders and business partners). Some additional practical pointers are provided in Part 8 to help this group maximise their tax relief.

I've also included a chapter for landlords. It explains how pension contributions can help reverse the tax increase you may suffer now that your mortgage interest is no longer tax deductible. The final chapter in Part 8 looks at the pros and cons of putting commercial property into a pension.

Part 9 answers a key family pension planning question: "Who should make the pension contributions: me or my spouse/partner?" There is also a chapter looking at the pros and cons of opening a pension for your children or grandchildren.

Future Changes to Pension Tax Relief?

Most of the content of this guide is based on the *current* tax rules affecting pensions. However, it's important to remember that pensions are long-term saving vehicles, which means some of the tax rules are likely to change while you are contributing to one.

For many years newspapers have been reporting that the Government plans to take away some of the tax incentives enjoyed by pension savers, in particular higher-rate tax relief. Fortunately there hasn't been any bad news recently. However, we wouldn't be surprised to see an announcement at some point in the future, simply because the public finances are in such a mess.

For this reason we believe that some individuals, such as higher-rate taxpayers, should make the most of the current tax incentives while they are still available. Other individuals, for example basic-rate taxpayers, could end up better off if there are changes.

Readers should bear all this in mind when we talk about things like the benefits and drawbacks of postponing pension contributions (Part 4 and Chapter 32). The tax rules could change!

Recent Tax Changes

In recent months there have been several announcements on the tax front that affect certain pension savers.

These include:

- Freezing the £50,270 higher-rate threshold until 6th April 2028
- The reduction in the additional-rate threshold from £150,000 to £125,140 on 6th April 2023
- Higher income tax rates on dividend income
- Raising the primary threshold for national insurance
- An increase in the rate of corporation tax

These changes affect pension savers in lots of different ways and are all covered in this new edition.

I hope you find *Pension Magic* an enjoyable and interesting read.

Scope of this Guide

This guide does not cover every aspect of pension saving. The focus is *maximising tax relief*, which is the main reason people invest in the first place. I do not cover issues like fees, how you should invest your money (in shares, property etc), or how to choose a pension provider. I make no excuses for these omissions. As it is, I've struggled to keep the guide to a manageable size focusing on tax saving strategies.

Nevertheless, it's important to point out that these other issues are extremely important. Annual account charges vary significantly from one pension provider to the next (from around 0.45% to 0.15%). If you invest in funds, the annual fees also vary considerably (for example, 0.95% for one popular managed fund compared with 0.08% for one well-known tracker fund). There's no point maximising the tax relief on your pension contributions if you give away all these savings over time in additional fees.

The focus of this guide is defined contribution pension schemes, also known as money purchase schemes. These include all individual pensions (for example, personal pensions and SIPPs) and most company pension schemes these days. The basic idea is you (and your employer if you have one) put money in and the amount of income you get out at the end of the day depends on how well your investments have performed.

There is very little discussion of defined benefit (final salary) pension schemes. With this type of scheme your employer promises to pay you a pension based on your salary and years of service. Final salary schemes are increasingly scarce in the private sector because employers are unwilling to guarantee to pay someone a set amount of income for the rest of their life. However, they are still the order of the day in the public sector, with the taxpayer picking up the tab.

Scottish Taxpayers

Pensions are all about income tax and income tax in Scotland is different to the rest of the UK. Most of the information in this guide is relevant to Scottish taxpayers. However, unless stated to the contrary, all examples and calculations are based on the assumption that the taxpayer concerned is not a Scottish taxpayer.

Finally, please remember that this guide is not meant to be a substitute for proper professional advice. Before you act you should contact either a suitably qualified accountant, tax advisor, IFA or pensions expert who understands your personal circumstances.

Part 1

Putting Money In:
The Pension Contribution Rules

Chapter 1

Tax Relief on Contributions: How it's Calculated

When you make pension contributions the taxman will top up your savings by paying cash directly into your plan. Effectively for every £80 you invest, the taxman will put in an extra £20.

Why £20, you might be asking? Well your contributions are treated as having been paid out of income that has already been taxed at the basic income tax rate of 20%. The taxman is therefore refunding the income tax you've already paid.

The company that manages your pension plan – usually an insurance company or SIPP provider – will claim this money for you from the taxman and credit it to your account.

So whatever contribution you make personally, divide it by 0.80 and you'll get the total amount that is invested in your pension pot.

Example
Peter invests £4,000 in a self-invested personal pension (SIPP). After the taxman makes his top-up payment, the total amount of money Peter will have sitting in his pension pot is £5,000:

$$£4,000/0.80 = £5,000$$

Basic-rate tax relief isn't the end of the story. If Peter is a *higher-rate* taxpayer, paying tax at 40%, he'll be able to claim even more tax relief.

The Cherry on Top – Higher Rate Relief

A higher-rate taxpayer is someone who earns more than £50,270.

If you are a higher-rate taxpayer the taxman will let you claim your higher-rate tax relief when you submit your tax return.

Alternatively, if you are a company employee, higher-rate tax relief can be provided immediately by reducing the tax paid on your salary via your PAYE code.

(See Chapter 5 for more information on how to claim higher-rate tax relief.)

Example
As we already know, Peter's personal contribution is £4,000 and total pension fund investment, including the taxman's top-up, is:

$$£4,000/0.80 = £5,000$$

The £4,000 is what's known as the 'net contribution' and the £5,000 is what's known as the 'gross contribution'.

Multiplying the gross contribution by 20% we get:

$$£5,000 \times 20\% = £1,000$$

This is Peter's higher-rate tax relief.

Effectively he has a pension investment of £5,000 which has cost him just £3,000 (£4,000 personal contribution less his £1,000 tax refund). In other words, he is getting all of his investments at a 40% discount.

This is the critical number. Being able to make investments year after year at a 40% discount can have a huge effect on the amount of wealth you accumulate.

Scottish Taxpayers 2022/23

The Scottish Parliament has the power to set income tax rates and thresholds for most types of income, most notably salaries, self-employment income, rental income and pensions. Interest and dividend income are still taxed using UK rates and thresholds.

Income tax in Scotland is being levied as follows in 2022/23:

£0 - £12,570	0%	Personal allowance (PA)
£12,570 - £14,732	19%	Starter rate
£14,732 - £25,688	20%	Basic rate
£25,688 - £43,662	21%	Intermediate rate
£43,662 - £150,000	41%	Higher rate
£150,000 +	46%	Top rate

Scottish taxpayers who pay tax at just 19%, or pay no tax at all, continue to enjoy 20% tax relief on their pension contributions.

Those who pay the 21% intermediate rate can claim the additional 1% tax relief by getting HMRC to adjust their tax code, completing a tax return or contacting HMRC. The same goes for those paying 41% tax or 46% tax.

National Insurance Relief?

Pensions provide income tax relief but generally no national insurance relief. However, it's important to point out that:

- Although there is generally no national insurance relief on pension contributions, there is also no national insurance payable on the income you withdraw from your pension. For example, someone who earns a salary of £50,000 in 2023/24 needs a pension of just £44,385 to end up with *exactly* the same after-tax income.

- If you are a higher-rate taxpayer your combined tax rate (income tax and national insurance) will be 42%. Pensions provide 40% tax relief which is pretty close to full tax relief.

- Although there is generally no national insurance relief on pension contributions, there is one important exception: salary sacrifice pensions. We cover these in detail in Part 6.

11

Summary

- When you make pension contributions you qualify for two types of income tax relief: Basic-rate tax relief which comes in the shape of top-ups to your pension plan and higher-rate relief which is normally claimed when you submit your tax return.

- Your total pension fund investment is found by dividing your personal contribution by 0.80. The taxman's top-up is paid directly to your pension provider who will credit your pension pot.

- Higher-rate relief is calculated by multiplying your gross pension fund contribution by 20%.

- Together these two tax reliefs mean all your pension investments come in at a 40% discount.

- There is generally no national insurance relief on pension contributions.

Chapter 2

How Much Can You Invest?

In this chapter we will examine the rules that determine how much you can invest in a pension each year.

Note that successive governments have continually tampered with the pension system, for better or worse. If you are making pension contributions over several decades you should not rely on the same set of rules applying in 5, 10 or 20 years' time.

The good news, for now at least, is that it's possible for most individuals to make big enough pension contributions and enjoy full income tax relief.

Age

This is a good one to kick off with. Generally anyone up to the ripe old age of 75 can make pension contributions.

In the March 2014 Budget the Government announced that it would explore whether this age limit should be changed or abolished. Following consultation, it was decided not to make any changes, so the age limit remains at 75.

There is effectively no lower age limit. You may not be able to set up your own pension plan if you're under 18 years of age but some pension providers have special products so that parents and grandparents can make pension contributions for their children and grandchildren (see Chapter 39 for more information).

Multiple Pension Schemes

A number of years ago many members of workplace schemes could not contribute to a second pension, such as a self-invested personal pension (SIPP). This is no longer the case.

Most people can now contribute to more than one pension and have more control over how their retirement savings are invested.

The Basic Pension Contribution Rule

To obtain tax relief on your pension contributions they have to stay within certain limits:

- **Earnings**. Contributions made by you *personally* must not exceed your annual earnings.

- **The £40,000 Annual Allowance.** Total pension contributions by you and anyone else (normally your employer) must not exceed £40,000 per year. The annual allowance is reduced once you start withdrawing certain types of income from your pension (see below). It may also be reduced if your "adjusted income" exceeds £240,000 (see Chapter 20 for more details).

Ignoring any pension contributions by the employer, an individual with earnings of £35,000 can contribute £35,000 to a pension with tax relief. An individual with earnings of £75,000 can contribute £40,000 (contributions capped by the annual allowance).

Employer contributions also have to be thrown into the mix when calculating the maximum pension contribution.

Let's say the individual with earnings of £75,000 is an employee and his employer contributes £10,000 to his pension. The maximum contribution he can make personally is £30,000:

£40,000 annual allowance – £10,000 from employer = £30,000

How Relevant Is this to Me?

Almost everyone making pension contributions needs to understand what is meant by the term 'earnings'. Earnings are not the same as income.

The annual allowance, on the other hand, does not affect most people because most of us do not have anything close to £40,000 paid into our pension plans each year. However, as we shall see in Part 4, there may be times when you want to make big catch-up contributions. In these circumstances it is important to know a bit more about how the annual allowance operates.

Gross vs Cash Contributions

The above pension contribution limits are for *gross* pension contributions. However, the money you actually pay into your pension is normally NOT a gross pension contribution (unless you belong to certain types of occupational pension scheme). To calculate your gross contributions you have to add on basic-rate tax relief (the taxman's top up). You do that by dividing your actual cash contribution by 0.80.

How does this affect the pension contribution limits? If you have earnings of £35,000 you cannot pay £35,000 into your pension plan and receive tax relief. You can only pay in £28,000 (£35,000 x 0.8). The taxman will add a further £7,000 in tax relief, bringing your total gross pension contribution to £35,000.

Similarly, the £40,000 annual allowance is a cap on total gross pension contributions. So the maximum cash pension contribution an individual can make in the absence of any employer contributions is £32,000 (£40,000 x 0.8), with the taxman adding a further £8,000 in tax relief.

Employer Contributions

Contributions by employers are always gross contributions. When your employer puts money into your pension plan there is no additional top up from the taxman. Instead the company obtains tax relief by claiming employee pension contributions as a tax deductible business expense.

So if your employer contributes £10,000 to your pension that will be a gross contribution and the maximum gross contribution you can make personally is £30,000:

$$£40,000 - £10,000 = £30,000$$

The maximum amount you can actually pay into your pension plan would then be £24,000:

$$£30,000 \times 0.8 = £24,000$$

You can only receive tax relief on this contribution if you have earnings of at least £30,000.

Occupational Pension Schemes

For many employees who belong to occupational schemes, the actual pension contribution is the same as the gross pension contribution.

Under the 'net pay arrangement' the employer deducts the employee's pension contributions from the employee's gross pay *before* tax is deducted. This means full tax relief is obtained immediately by paying the contribution out of pre-tax income. There is no top up by the taxman and no need to claim higher-rate tax relief via a tax return.

(Similarly, Scottish employees who pay tax at 21% or more do not have to claim back their additional tax relief from HMRC if they belong to a net pay arrangement – see previous chapter.)

Not all contributions by employees are made gross. If the employer has a pension scheme that uses 'relief at source' (usually group personal pensions), the employee's contributions are paid after the employee's salary has been taxed. Basic-rate relief is then claimed by the pension scheme and added to the member's pension pot to obtain their total gross pension contribution.

Earnings

To obtain tax relief on your pension contributions you have to have earnings – 'relevant UK earnings' to be precise.

Employees

If you are an employee, your relevant UK earnings will include:

- Salary or wages
- Bonus, overtime, and commissions, and
- Taxable benefits in kind.

There are a few other bits and bobs that can count as relevant UK earnings for pension contribution purposes, including redundancy payments that exceed the £30,000 tax-free threshold and statutory sick pay and statutory maternity pay.

Company Directors

Most small company owners are also directors. For pension contribution purposes company directors are treated just like regular employees. Their relevant UK earnings include their salary, bonus, overtime, commissions and taxable benefits in kind.

As shareholders of their companies they can also pay themselves dividends. To save tax and national insurance, many company owners take a small tax-free salary and the rest of their income as dividends.

It is often tax efficient for company owners to pay themselves a salary equal to the national insurance primary threshold (£11,908 for 2022/23) and take the rest of their income as dividends (see Chapter 31).

The problem, however, is that dividends are NOT earnings. As such, a company director with a salary of £11,908 and dividends of £50,000 can only contribute £11,908 to a pension with tax relief.

The actual cash contribution would be £9,526 (£11,908 x 0.8) with the taxman adding £2,382 in tax relief for a gross contribution of £11,908.

Fortunately for company owners, they can get their companies to make pension contributions (employer contributions) and these are not restricted to their earnings (although they are restricted by the £40,000 annual allowance). We'll take a closer look at pension planning for company owners in Part 7.

The Self-Employed

Most people would regard any business owner as 'self-employed'. However, when HMRC talks about 'self-employed' individuals they are referring specifically to owners of unincorporated businesses, in other words businesses that are not companies.

The most common are sole traders (one-person businesses) and partnerships.

If you are a sole trader your relevant UK earnings are generally the pre-tax profits of the business. If you are a partner, your relevant UK earnings will be your share of the partnership's pre-tax profit.

The problem is that many self-employed individuals don't know what their pre-tax profits are!

Many have an accounting period that is the same as the tax year, running to 5th April each year or 31st March. This can create a practical problem when it comes to maximising tax relief on pension contributions.

Although most salary earners (including company directors) have earnings that are fairly predictable (their salaries), the exact profits on which self-employed business owners can base their pension contributions may not be known until the accounts are drawn up *after* the tax year has ended.

In other words, as a self-employed business owner you may only know what your relevant UK earnings are when it is too late to make pension contributions. You cannot make back-dated pension contributions after the tax year has ended.

Income but Not Earnings

Earnings do not include:

- Rental income
- Interest
- Dividends
- Capital gains

For example, if you have earnings of £30,000 and rental income of £20,000 from buy-to-let properties, the maximum gross pension contribution you can make with tax relief is £30,000.

With regards to rental income, there is one exception. When it comes to tax, owners of furnished holiday lettings are treated quite differently to other rental property owners and pensions are no exception. Profits from furnished holiday lettings count as relevant UK earnings for pension purposes.

Individuals with No Earnings

Some people don't have any earnings, including non-working spouses and minor children.

Many professional landlords, who derive all of their income from rental properties, will also not have any earnings.

The good news is that everyone under the age of 75 can make a pension contribution of £3,600 per year, regardless of earnings. The actual cash contribution would be £2,880, with the taxman adding £720 to bring the total gross contribution to £3,600.

We'll take a closer look at the pros and cons of making pension contributions when you have no earnings in Part 9.

The Annual Allowance

The annual allowance is the overall cap on the amount of pension contributions you can make with tax relief. It's currently £40,000 and has been fixed at this level since April 2014. We don't expect it to be increased to compensate for inflation.

Your annual allowance is reduced once you start withdrawing certain types of income from your pension (see below).

Your annual allowance is also reduced if your "adjusted income" exceeds £240,000 (see Chapter 20 for more details).

The annual allowance includes pension contributions made by both you and anyone else (normally your employer).

If your contributions do exceed the annual allowance, you can carry forward unused allowance from the three previous tax years.

If the annual allowance is exceeded, and the excess is not covered by carry forward, the excess is taxed at your marginal income tax rate (20%, 40% or 45%).

This annual allowance charge can be paid when you submit your tax return or deducted from your pension savings if it's over £2,000.

Those who have to be most careful about the annual allowance are those making big one-off pension contributions. Another group that has to be careful are members of final salary pension schemes (also known as defined benefit pension schemes). The value of their pension benefits can increase by significantly more than £40,000 in the year they receive a substantial pay increase. Professional advice should also be obtained in these circumstances.

The annual allowance is generous enough for most people. However, the fact that it has been frozen at £40,000 for so many years, coupled with rising inflation, means that more and more people are likely to find it restricts their retirement saving.

Pension Input Periods

Up until a few years ago, when calculating whether the annual allowance was exceeded, you didn't count pension contributions made during a *tax year* (5th April to 6th April). Instead you used the pension scheme's annual *pension input period*.

As a result, quite big pension contributions made during two different tax years could have fallen into just one pension input period and exceeded the annual allowance.

However, with effect from 6th April 2016 all pension input periods are now aligned with the tax year.

The Carry Forward Rule

If you want to make a big pension contribution that exceeds the annual allowance you can tap any unused allowance from the three previous tax years.

This means that someone who hasn't made any pension contributions so far during the current tax year can potentially make a pension contribution of up to £160,000 in 2022/23 and enjoy full tax relief:

- £40,000 for 2022/23
- £40,000 for 2021/22
- £40,000 for 2020/21
- £40,000 for 2019/20

Example

Paula is a sole trader and makes bumper profits of £160,000 during the 2022/23 tax year.

She transfers £80,000 into her pension plan, resulting in a gross pension contribution of £100,000 (£80,000/0.8).

Her gross pension contributions in the three previous tax years were:

	Pension Contribution	Unused Annual Allowance
2021/22	£20,000	£20,000
2020/21	£20,000	£20,000
2019/20	£10,000	£30,000

In total Paula has £70,000 of unused annual allowance.

Together with the £40,000 annual allowance for the current tax year, Paula can make a total gross pension contribution of up to £110,000.

Her £100,000 gross pension contribution is therefore within the limits and does not exceed her earnings and therefore enjoys full tax relief.

You use the annual allowance for the current tax year first. You then use your unused annual allowance from the *earliest* tax year first (2019/20 in Paula's case).

This leaves any unused allowance from the most recent tax years free to be carried forward.

In Paula's case she will be able to carry forward £10,000 of unused allowance from 2021/22 and use it in a future tax year.

Earnings Can't Be Carried Forward

To enjoy tax relief, the pension contributions you make personally cannot exceed your earnings for the current tax year.

Although you can carry forward unused annual allowance, you cannot carry forward earnings from previous years or make backdated pension contributions.

Membership of a Pension Scheme Required

Unused annual allowance can only be carried forward if you were a member of a registered pension scheme for the period in question.

For example, if you start contributing to a pension now but did not belong to any pension scheme in the three previous tax years, you cannot carry forward any unused annual allowance from those years.

On a practical level, this means that someone who does not currently have a pension plan in place, but may wish to make big contributions in a few years' time, should consider setting one up as soon as possible.

Getting your Contribution Right

The pension contribution rules are quite complex... but only if you have quite big contributions and are in danger of exceeding the annual allowance.

Most people will not have £40,000 per year added to their pension pots and are unaffected by the annual allowance rules (individuals who want to make big catch-up contributions are an important exception – see Chapter 18).

The earnings limit is also irrelevant for the vast majority of people. Most would never contemplate contributing anything close to 100% of their earnings to a pension. (Company directors are one exception because they often pay themselves a small tax-free salary and therefore have very low 'earnings'.)

I don't want to sound flippant but it's important not to become bogged down by rules that may never affect you. Calculating the maximum pension contribution you *can* make is not the important issue for most people. What is far more important is calculating the maximum pension contribution you *should* make.

A far more important calculation for many individuals is the maximum contribution that will obtain full higher-rate tax relief. This is the subject of Chapter 4.

Contributions after Withdrawals Have Started

When you start withdrawing income from your pension your ability to make further pension contributions could be severely restricted.

You may no longer be entitled to a £40,000 annual allowance. Instead your contributions could be subject to the 'money purchase annual allowance'.

The money purchase annual allowance is just £4,000.

There are other anti-avoidance rules designed to prevent money being taken out of a pension in order to make new pension contributions, thereby benefiting from two rounds of tax relief.

If you use your tax-free lump sum to significantly increase your pension contributions, the contributions may fall foul of HMRC's recycling rules and a tax charge of up to 70% could be imposed.

We'll take a closer look at both these issues in Part 2 which deals with taking money out of pensions.

Chapter 3

The Lifetime Allowance

The lifetime allowance is the maximum amount of money you are allowed to save up in pensions with full tax relief.

In 2012 it was reduced from £1.8 million to £1.5 million and then to £1.25 million and finally to £1 million. The Government then promised to increase the lifetime allowance with inflation and kept its promise for just two years!

The lifetime allowance is currently £1,073,100 and will remain at this level until the end of the 2025/26 tax year.

This freeze to the lifetime allowance was announced as part of the Government's plan to raise taxes sneakily by allowing inflation to erode the value of various tax allowances. Fortunately, the freeze was not extended for a further two years in the November 2022 Autumn Statement, unlike many other tax thresholds.

If your pension savings exceed the lifetime allowance you will have to pay the lifetime allowance charge on the excess.

The lifetime allowance charge is 55% if the excess funds are paid out as a lump sum (this is only possible before age 75). The tax charge is 25% if the excess funds are retained inside the pension plan, with income tax also payable on any withdrawals.

Basic-rate taxpayers will usually be better off withdrawing the excess funds as taxable income because the overall tax rate will be 40% instead of 55%. Higher-rate taxpayers will pay roughly the same amount of tax on excess lump sums and income. However, paying the 25% charge may be preferable so that the money can continue to grow tax free inside the pension plan and stay outside the inheritance tax net (see Chapter 10).

In this chapter I will not spend too much time explaining how the lifetime allowance charge is applied in practice if your pension savings go over the limit. Instead I will try to answer the more important questions: Are my pension savings likely to exceed the lifetime allowance? If so, does it really matter?

How is the Lifetime Allowance Applied?

Your pension savings will be tested against the lifetime allowance when there is a "benefit crystallisation event" – typically when you start withdrawing money, even if it's just your tax-free lump sum.

The lifetime allowance test also takes place if you reach age 75 with pension savings that haven't been touched yet.

If you place your pension into drawdown when you retire you may face a second lifetime allowance test when you reach age 75.

(You may also face this second lifetime allowance test if you use your drawdown funds to later buy an annuity.)

This second test may affect you if your drawdown fund has grown in size, for example if you've continued working and haven't withdrawn much money from it or have enjoyed very high investment returns.

But if your drawdown fund has fallen in value (for example, if you've been withdrawing money steadily) there will be nothing additional to measure against the lifetime allowance.

Example
Saul is 65 and has a pension fund worth £800,000. In 2022/23 he takes a tax-free lump sum of £200,000 and moves the remaining £600,000 into drawdown. The lifetime allowance is £1,073,100 so Saul does not have to pay the lifetime allowance charge. With an £800,000 pension pot this benefit crystallisation event uses up 75% of his lifetime allowance, leaving him with 25% for future use.

He keeps working and doesn't withdraw any income from his drawdown fund. 10 years later his drawdown fund has grown from £600,000 to £1 million. Because he's now 75 there's a second lifetime allowance test. The amount crystallised is the current value of his drawdown fund less its original value: £1 million - £600,000 = £400,000.

Let's assume that when Saul is 75 the lifetime allowance has increased to £1.3 million. Saul is entitled to 25% of this, i.e. £325,000. Thus Saul will face a lifetime allowance charge on £75,000 (£400,000 minus £325,000). The excess funds are subject to a lifetime allowance charge of 25% (£18,750) and he can withdraw the rest as taxable income.

Note, in this example we have assumed that the lifetime allowance increases again from the start of the 2026/27 tax year. This is by no means certain. Perhaps the Government will freeze it for longer if it is concerned about the public finances.

It should be fairly easy for Saul to avoid the lifetime allowance charge altogether by simply withdrawing enough money before he is 75. He should withdraw the amount his drawdown fund has grown over and above his remaining lifetime allowance.

Because the withdrawals will be subject to income tax he may be better off doing this over several tax years to avoid paying tax at 40% or more.

Am I in Danger of Exceeding the Lifetime Allowance?

Arguably those most at risk of going over the lifetime allowance are long-serving members of final salary pension schemes. The annual pension you receive is generally multiplied by 20 and added to any additional lump sum you receive.

For example, with a lifetime allowance of £1,073,100, someone retiring with a final salary pension of more than £53,655 per year (with no separate lump sum) could be subject to the lifetime allowance charge (£53,655 x 20 = £1,073,100).

It's also possible that some members of modern occupational pension schemes in the private sector and those with SIPPs and personal pensions will breach the lifetime allowance.

Members of these "money purchase" pension schemes could end up paying the lifetime allowance charge if they have made successful investments, saved hard or received generous contributions from their employers.

However, it's vital to stress that most people are in danger of saving <u>too little</u>, not too much, in pensions.

Table 1 will give you some idea whether you're in danger of exceeding the lifetime allowance. The table shows approximately how many years it will take your existing pension pot and annual contributions to exceed the lifetime allowance.

Table 1
Number of Years until
Lifetime Allowance Exceeded

Current Pot	Annual Gross Pension Contribution								
	£0k	£5k	£10k	£15k	£20k	£25k	£30	£35k	£40k
£0k	n/a	46	35	28	24	21	19	18	17
£100k	44	33	27	23	20	18	16	15	15
£150k	36	28	24	20	18	16	15	14	13
£200k	31	25	21	18	16	15	14	13	12
£250k	26	22	19	17	15	13	12	11	11
£300k	23	19	17	15	13	12	11	10	10
£400k	17	15	13	12	11	10	9	9	8
£500k	13	12	10	9	9	8	7	7	7
£600k	10	9	8	7	7	6	6	5	5
£700k	7	6	6	5	5	5	4	4	4
£800k	5	4	4	4	4	3	3	3	3
£900k	3	3	3	2	2	2	2	2	2
£1m	1	1	1	1	1	1	1	1	1

Example

Ann is 50, has pension savings of £100,000 and is making an annual pension contribution of £10,000. The table tells us her pension pot will exceed the lifetime allowance in roughly 27 years' time.

Ann intends to stop working and start withdrawing money from her pension in just 10 years' time, when she is 60. So the lifetime allowance probably does not pose any risk to her.

A much more relevant question is: Will Ann's pension pot be big enough to retire on? In 10 years' time she will have pension savings of roughly £370,000 which seems a bit on the low side to me, unless she has a spouse or partner who also has pension savings.

(Note, if you reach age 75 with uncrystallised (untouched) pension savings, those savings will be tested against the lifetime allowance at age 75. So in practice the maximum amount of time before Ann's pension pot will be tested is 25 years, not 27 years.)

27

Table 1 Assumptions

The figures in Table 1 were calculated by making the following assumptions:

- The lifetime allowance is frozen until 2026/27 and then increases by 2% per year (the assumed very long-term rate of inflation). Remember, the Government could do the opposite: freeze or reduce the lifetime allowance

- Annual pension contributions also increase by 2% per year

- Once annual contributions reach £40,000 (the level of the annual allowance) there are no further increases

- The annual allowance is not affected by the restriction for those with over £240,000 adjusted income (see Chapter 20)

- Annual pension contributions include contributions by both the individual and any employer and also include basic-rate tax relief (the taxman's top up)

- Pension investments grow by 7.5% per year. With 2% inflation this equates to a real return of roughly 5.5% per year which is roughly what the UK stock market has delivered since 1900

It should be stressed that, when doing calculations like these that cover long periods of time, the outcome can be altered dramatically by tweaking the numbers just slightly.

For example, the last assumption possibly overstates future investment returns by ignoring fees and charges. If net investment returns are lower than 7.5%, it will take longer to exceed the lifetime allowance than the table suggests.

For example, let's say you have a pension pot of £200,000 and pension contributions of £15,000 per year. Table 1 tells us that you will exceed the lifetime allowance in roughly 18 years' time.

But if your investments grow by just 5% per year it will take around 26 years to exceed the lifetime allowance. And if your investments grow by 10% per year it will take around 15 years to exceed the lifetime allowance.

Some of the other assumptions could also be called into question. For example, there's a good chance your salary and therefore your pension contributions will grow faster than inflation as you climb the career ladder. If so your pension pot will exceed the lifetime allowance sooner than the table suggests.

It may also be unreasonable to assume that the annual allowance will never increase above £40,000. Surely it must go up at some point to compensate for inflation? Possibly, but it's just as likely to be cut by a Government that wants to collect more tax.

Finally, assuming a long-term inflation rate of 2% per year seemed reasonable when it first appeared in this guide. But with inflation currently running at over 10% this assumption may now seem a bit out of touch. Having said this, nobody knows what the average inflation rate will be over the next, say, 10 years. If inflation turns out to be higher, the lifetime allowance may increase faster, making it less of a threat to pension savers than the table suggests. But higher inflation may also lead to higher nominal investment returns and thus bigger pension pots, which are more likely to exceed the lifetime allowance. Overall, it's difficult to make concrete statements about higher inflation and the danger of exceeding the lifetime allowance.

Small Pension Pot, Big Catch Up Contributions

Let's say you haven't saved up much money in a pension yet and want to make big catch up contributions.

The table tells us that someone who doesn't have one penny of pension savings and saves the maximum amount of £40,000 per year will exceed the lifetime allowance after just 17 years.

This won't be a problem if the individual is getting closer to retirement and wants to start withdrawing money within the next 17 years (for example, those in their late forties or older).

It may be a problem if you are younger. For example, if you are 35 your pension savings will exceed the lifetime allowance not too long after your 50th birthday. By the time you reach the minimum retirement age (probably 57 – see Chapter 7), there's a good chance your pension savings will be well in excess of the lifetime allowance.

Big Pension Pot, No More Pension Contributions

The first column of Table 1 shows roughly how long it will take to exceed the lifetime allowance even if you stop making pension contributions.

For example, someone who currently has a £400,000 pension pot and stops making contributions will exceed the lifetime allowance in around 17 years' time. This may not be a problem if you are in your forties or older but it may be a problem if you are in your thirties.

Postponing the Lifetime Allowance Charge

It is possible to postpone the lifetime allowance charge by crystallising just enough of your pension savings to remain within the lifetime allowance.

For example, let's say when you reach the minimum retirement age you have a pension pot of £1.5 million and the lifetime allowance is £1.25 million. You decide to crystallise £1.25 million by taking a tax-free lump sum of £312,500 and moving the remaining £937,500 into drawdown where it can continue to grow tax free.

Because the amount crystallised does not exceed the lifetime allowance, no lifetime allowance charge will be payable. The remaining £250,000 will continue to grow tax free until further benefits are taken (or you reach age 75). At this point the lifetime allowance charge will be payable.

How Bad Is the Lifetime Allowance Charge?

For several years now I have argued that financial commentators spend far too much time fretting about the annual allowance and the lifetime allowance when the vast majority of people are unaffected by these restrictions.

Even if your pension savings do exceed the lifetime allowance it's not the end of the world. The charge is not as high as it first appears and your excess pension savings will still enjoy other tax benefits, including tax-free growth and protection from inheritance tax.

If you do have to pay the lifetime allowance charge you may end up no worse off than someone who puts their money in an ISA (the main alternative tax shelter).

Example

Justus invests an extra £800 in his pension and the taxman adds £200 of basic-rate tax relief, giving him a gross pension contribution of £1,000. He also receives higher-rate tax relief of £200 which means the £1,000 investment costs him just £600. Let's also assume that Justus's friend Kevin invests £600 in an ISA – the exact same amount Justus invests personally (taking into account his higher-rate tax relief).

Now let's look at what happens when Justus and Kevin withdraw this money. To keep the example simple we can ignore investment growth because both pensions and ISAs enjoy exactly the same tax-free growth.

However, let's assume that Justus's £1,000 pension contribution takes him over the lifetime allowance by exactly £1,000. After paying the 25% lifetime allowance charge (£250) and 20% income tax on the remaining £750 withdrawal Justus is left with £600.

Withdrawals from Kevin's ISA are tax free so he is left with £600 – exactly the same amount as Justus who had to pay the lifetime allowance charge.

What this example reveals is that:

Even if you have to pay the lifetime allowance charge you will end up in exactly the same position as someone who puts their money in an ISA.

In the above example I assumed that Justus is a basic-rate taxpayer when he retires. If he is a higher-rate taxpayer and pays 40% income tax on the £750 of income he withdraws he will be left with just £450. Kevin the ISA investor will then have 33% more money than Justus the pension investor. In this case Justus would be better off putting his money in an ISA.

However, because Justus can decide how much he withdraws from his pension and when, he may be able to keep his income below the higher-rate threshold (which is currently £50,270).

Should You Try to Avoid the Charge?

Nobody wants to pay tax unnecessarily but clearly the lifetime allowance charge isn't something you should lose sleep over. Having a pension pot of over £1 million is something to celebrate.

It's important that you do not do something harmful just to avoid the lifetime allowance charge:

- Do not opt out of your workplace pension if that means giving up pension contributions from your employer (which are effectively free money).

- Do not try to limit your investment returns just to stay below the lifetime allowance. After all, it's better to pay 25% tax than have nothing to tax at all. If you want to place your pension savings into less risky investments that's a different matter, however.

- Do not stop making pension contributions too early – it's probably better to overshoot and have a pension pot that is slightly larger than the lifetime allowance than one which is below the lifetime allowance.

Protecting Your Lifetime Allowance

If you think you may have more than £1 million of pension savings by the time you retire or reach age 75 you may wish to register for "protection".

There are two types of protection you can apply for:

- Fixed protection 2016
- Individual protection 2016

Fixed protection 2016 fixes your lifetime allowance at £1.25 million. To qualify you and your employer must not have made any pension contributions after 5th April 2016 (or have accrued benefits in a final salary scheme).

For individual protection 2016 the value of your pension savings must be more than £1 million on 5th April 2016. It fixes your lifetime allowance at the lower of £1.25 million or the value of your pensions on 5th April 2016.

It is possible to make further pension contributions after that date.

You can apply online for both types of protection:

www.gov.uk/guidance/pension-schemes-protect-your-lifetime-allowance

There is no deadline to apply for either type of protection, although you must apply before you withdraw money from your pension.

Could the Lifetime Allowance be Reduced?

In June 2021 there were rumours circulating in various newspapers that the lifetime allowance could be reduced to just £900,000 or even £800,000, to help the Government cover the cost of the pandemic.

At the time of writing nothing has been announced but we wouldn't be surprised if such a change is made at some point. It would be ill conceived and discourage retirement saving... but successive governments have found it impossible not to tinker with the pension tax rules.

If the lifetime allowance is reduced we would expect there to be protection for those whose pension pots exceed the new limit.

Final Words on the Lifetime Allowance

The lifetime allowance receives a lot of press coverage and for those affected it is an important consideration.

However, the reality is that most people are in danger of saving *too little* in pensions, not too much.

Throughout this guide I therefore assume that the reader is not in any danger of breaching the lifetime allowance. If you think you may be affected, you should consider speaking to a financial advisor about your options.

Chapter 4

How to Maximise Your Higher-Rate Tax Relief

Everyone who makes pension contributions enjoys basic-rate tax relief (the taxman's 20% top up). If you are a higher-rate taxpayer you can also claim an additional 20% tax relief.

However, some higher-rate taxpayers don't enjoy full tax relief on their pension contributions because they don't understand how higher-rate relief is calculated. It's a bit like paying for a business class ticket and accidentally sitting in economy.

What is a Higher-Rate Taxpayer?

A higher-rate taxpayer is someone with taxable income of more than £50,270 (see below for Scottish taxpayers). The threshold normally increases with inflation but has been fixed for seven years until the end of the 2027/28 tax year on 5th April 2028.

This means that many basic-rate taxpayers will become higher-taxpayers, even if their incomes simply increase because of inflation. Similarly, individuals who are already higher-rate taxpayers will see an even larger chunk of their incomes taxed at 40%, even though they are no better off in real terms.

On a more positive note, many pension savers will be able to protect themselves from this tax increase by making pension contributions which enjoy higher-rate tax relief.

How Is Higher-Rate Relief Calculated?

When you make pension contributions the taxman gives you a bigger basic-rate band which means more of your income is taxed at 20% instead of 40%.

Your basic-rate band is increased by the same amount as your *gross* pension contributions.

Example

Sandy is a sole trader with pre-tax profits of £57,000. He has £6,730 of income taxed at 40% (£57,000 - £50,270).

He puts £5,000 into a pension. The taxman adds £1,250 of basic-rate relief for a gross contribution of £6,250 (£5,000/0.8).

To calculate his higher-rate relief his basic-rate band is increased by £6,250, allowing £6,250 of income to be taxed at 20% instead of 40%. This saves Sandy £1,250 in tax (£6,250 x 20%).

This is the best possible outcome. Sandy has received basic-rate and higher-rate tax relief on his entire pension contribution. In total he enjoys 40% tax relief:

$$(£1,250 + £1,250) / £6,250 = 40\%$$

The Maximum Higher Rate Relief

The maximum higher-rate tax relief you can claim is:

Your Gross Pension Contribution x 20%

However, you will only enjoy the maximum higher-rate tax relief if you have at least this much income taxed at 40%.

If your income is £50,270 plus one pound, you will only get higher-rate tax relief on one pound of pension contributions.

Sandy, whose income is £57,000, can enjoy higher-rate tax relief on a gross pension contribution of up to £6,730 (£57,000 – £50,270). His actual gross pension contribution is £6,250 so he has stayed within the limits. If he contributes more than £6,730, the additional contribution will only receive basic-rate relief.

Tax Planning

Big pension contributions can be a bad idea if you don't have enough income taxed at 40%.

To enjoy the maximum tax relief you may wish to consider spreading your pension contributions over a number of tax years.

If maximising tax relief is your priority, you should make sure your gross pension contributions do not exceed the amount of income you have taxed at 40%.

Example revisited

Sandy is a sole trader with pre-tax profits of £57,000. He has £6,730 of income taxed at 40% (£57,000 - £50,270 higher-rate threshold).

Sandy puts £15,000 into his pension. The taxman adds £3,750 of basic-rate relief. His gross contribution is £18,750 (£15,000/0.8).

His basic-rate band is increased by £18,750 which means his maximum higher-rate tax relief is:

$$£18,750 \times 20\% = £3,750$$

However, Sandy does not have £18,750 of income taxed at 40%, he only has £6,730. So the actual higher-rate relief he will receive is:

$$£6,730 \times 20\% = £1,346$$

Although his basic-rate band has been increased significantly, he doesn't have enough income to use it! Sandy is only obtaining higher-rate tax relief on £6,730 worth of pension contributions. In total he enjoys just 27% tax relief:

$$(£3,750 + £1,346) / £18,750 = 27\%$$

What can Sandy do if he wants to enjoy the maximum higher-rate relief? He can spread his contributions over several tax years.

If he wants to invest £15,000 (£18,750 gross) and if we assume he has around £6,730 of income per year taxed at 40%, this means he could consider spreading his gross contributions over three tax years:

Year 1	£6,730
Year 2	£6,730
Year 3	£5,290

Table 2
Maximising Higher-Rate Tax Relief:
Maximum Pension Contributions 2022/23

Taxable Income £	Maximum Gross Contribution £	Maximum Cash Contribution £
50,270	0	0
55,000	4,730	3,784
60,000	9,730	7,784
65,000	14,730	11,784
70,000	19,730	15,784
75,000	24,730	19,784
80,000	29,730	23,784
85,000	34,730	27,784
90,000	39,730	31,784
95,000	44,730	35,784
100,000	49,730	39,784

Note: A gross contribution of more than £40,000 is only possible if you have unused annual allowance from the three previous tax years.

Rule of Thumb

If maximising tax relief is your priority, the maximum amount you should contribute to a pension in the current tax year is:

Your taxable income minus *£50,270*

This is your maximum *gross* pension contribution. Multiply this number by 0.8 to obtain the maximum amount you can actually invest (your net cash contribution).

Table 2 contains some sample maximum pension contributions for different levels of income. Although you can contribute up to £40,000 per year (ignoring any employer contributions), only someone with income of £90,270 or more would enjoy full higher-rate tax relief on such a large gross contribution:

£90,270 - £50,270 = £40,000

Someone with income over £90,270 can contribute more than £40,000 and enjoy higher-rate tax relief on the entire contribution. However, to do this in practice they would have to carry forward unused annual allowance from previous tax years.

Big Contributions Close to Retirement

When you are close to retirement it may be worth making pension contributions that are larger than normal, even if you only enjoy basic-rate tax relief.

This is because it is possible to withdraw all the extra money you contribute immediately after you retire and 25% will be tax free.

We'll take a look at the potential tax savings in Chapter 11.

Taxpayers with Dividend Income

Some taxpayers whose *non-dividend* income is close to the £50,270 higher-rate threshold may not enjoy full higher-rate relief on their pension contributions if they also have dividend income.

Example
In 2022/23 Alistair has salary and rental income of £50,270. He also has dividend income of £5,000. His dividend income all falls over the higher-rate threshold but the first £2,000 of this is tax free thanks to the dividend allowance.

If Alistair makes a gross pension contribution of £3,000 his basic-rate band will be increased by £3,000. However, we know that £2,000 of his dividend income is tax free no matter which tax band it falls into. A further £1,000 will be taxed at 8.75% instead of 33.75%, saving him £250 (25%). So Alistair's total higher-rate relief comes to £250 which is just one third the maximum relief of £750 (£3,000 x 25%).

This example will only be relevant to a small number of taxpayers. Nevertheless, what it reveals is that you will not enjoy full higher-rate tax relief on your pension contributions if the first £2,000 of your dividend income falls into your increased basic-rate band.

Higher-Rate Taxpayers in Scotland

As we saw in Chapter 1, Scotland has more income tax bands than the rest of the UK. However, the biggest increase occurs when your income rises above £43,662. At this point you become a higher-rate taxpayer and your income tax rate jumps from 21% to 41%.

So if you're a Scottish taxpayer, the maximum amount you should contribute to a pension if you want full higher-rate relief is:

Your taxable income <u>minus</u> *£43,662*

For example, a Scottish taxpayer who earns £50,000 can make a gross pension contribution of £6,338. This includes 20% basic-rate tax relief so the net cash contribution would be £5,070 (£6,338 x 0.8).

As a higher-rate taxpayer (paying 41% tax) an extra £1,331 of tax relief can then be claimed back (£6,338 x 21%).

Remember the Scottish Parliament can tax most types of income but NOT interest and dividends. So if you are a company owner in Scotland and pay yourself a small salary and the rest of your income comes in the shape of dividends, the relevant higher-rate threshold is the "Westminster" one – £50,270. (See Chapter 31 for more on how company directors structure their pay.)

Example

Angus is a sole trader based in Scotland with taxable income of £46,000 in 2022/23. Angus can make a gross pension contribution of £2,338 (£46,000 - £43,662) with full higher-rate tax relief.

Douglas is a company director/shareholder based in Scotland with the same amount of taxable income (£46,000) but made up mostly of dividends. If Douglas makes a pension contribution of £2,338 he will not enjoy any higher-rate tax relief because he is not a higher-rate taxpayer (the UK, not Scottish, higher-rate threshold applies to his dividend income).

Chapter 5

How to Claim Higher-Rate Tax Relief

Scottish Widows once reported that up to a quarter of higher-rate taxpayers did not claim all the tax relief they were entitled to.

Many taxpayers believe incorrectly that all of their pension tax relief is automatically credited to their pension pots.

Those who usually do NOT have to claim higher-rate tax relief are members of occupational money purchase pension schemes. Their pension contributions are paid out of their salaries before tax is deducted, so full 40% tax relief is effectively granted immediately.

Those who are affected include members of group personal pensions, group stakeholder pensions and group SIPPs. With these arrangements the contributions are made out of after-tax pay, so tax relief has to be actively claimed.

Individuals with their own private pension plans also have to actively claim their higher-rate tax relief.

Gross vs Net Contributions

Another mistake made by higher-rate taxpayers when completing tax returns is entering net cash pension contributions (the amount they actually pay in), instead of their gross contributions (which include the taxman's basic-rate tax relief top up).

Page 4 of your tax return is for 'Tax reliefs'. Box 1 asks for:

Payments to registered pension schemes where basic rate tax relief will be claimed by your pension provider (called 'relief at source'). Enter the payments and basic rate tax

If you personally pay £3,000 into your pension and insert this number on your tax return, the taxman will give you £600 of higher-rate tax relief:

$$£3,000 \times 20\% = £600$$

But if you enter the correct amount, which is £3,750 (£3,000/0.8), the taxman will give you £750 of higher-rate tax relief:

$$£3,750 \times 20\% = £750$$

Do not include employer pension contributions.

Backdated Claims

If you have not claimed your higher-rate tax relief, the good news is you can make a backdated claim going back four years. Rebates can run to thousands of pounds.

Write to your local tax office, outlining the gross contributions you have made and the tax years they relate to, or speak to an accountant.

How to Claim Higher-Rate Tax Relief

The standard way to claim higher-rate tax relief is when you submit your tax return. You can also claim it through an adjustment to your tax code. This allows tax relief to be provided immediately because less tax will be deducted from your salary each month.

(A tax code is used by your employer to calculate the amount of tax to deduct from your pay. If you have the wrong tax code you could end up paying too much or too little tax.)

You can have your tax code adjusted by contacting HMRC and some pension companies provide template letters for this purpose.

You may need to contact HMRC again if your pension contributions increase, for example if you receive a pay increase or if you make one-off contributions during the year.

Chapter 6

Will Higher-Rate Tax Relief Be Scrapped?

For many years now there have been fears the Government will take away the additional tax relief enjoyed by higher-rate taxpayers on their pension contributions.

Up until now this has been done *indirectly* by reducing the annual allowance from £255,000 to £40,000 and this allowance has remained frozen for many years.

A clamp down on high earners came into effect in 2016 with the introduction of the tapered annual allowance (see Chapter 20).

David Cameron's government consulted on whether to completely reform pension tax relief and an announcement was expected in the March 2016 Budget. However, in that Budget speech Chancellor George Osborne stated that "it was clear there is no consensus" and pension tax relief was left unchanged. Apparently the decision to leave pension tax relief alone was made so as not to antagonize voters ahead of the EU referendum!

A little bit later there were newspaper reports that George Osborne's successor, Philip Hammond, had made cutting pension tax relief a priority, following his embarrassing u-turn over national insurance for the self-employed, which left a hole in the public finances.

However, in July 2017, while speaking to the Association of British Insurers, Secretary of State for Work and Pensions David Gauke apparently said that he did not expect to see any fundamental changes to pension tax relief in the near future.

The pensions industry took comfort from this comment but then in February 2020 there was fresh speculation that former Chancellor Sajid Javid was considering cutting higher-rate tax relief. He resigned before he could cause any damage and was replaced as Chancellor by Rishi Sunak.

In his March 2020 Budget speech Rishi Sunak made no mention of higher-rate tax relief and instead increased the income thresholds where the tapered annual allowance applies (see Chapter 20). This has helped those with high income to benefit from the £40,000 annual allowance, without any reduction.

Before the March 2021 Budget there were, once again, rumours doing the rounds that the Government would scrap higher-rate tax relief or launch some sort of consultation. To everyone's relief no such announcement was made.

In June 2021 the *Telegraph* newspaper reported that the Government was considering replacing higher-rate tax relief with a flat rate of tax relief for everyone (possibly around 30%), with an announcement expected in the 2021 Autumn Statement. Once again no such announcement was made.

The rumours were again circulating ahead of the November 2022 Autumn Statement with one tabloid newspaper boldly stating that: "Prime Minister Rishi Sunak and Chancellor Jeremy Hunt are lining up yet another pensions tax raid... Finally, it looks like it's going to happen, with Ministers preparing to cut relief for higher earners. It may be slashed from 40 percent or 45 percent to just 20 percent, in line with basic-rate tax relief".

What was announced this time round? Absolutely nothing.

Of course changes to pension tax relief could take place at some point in the future to help pay for the Government's eye-watering £400 billion covid spending splurge and the billions currently being spent to help households with their energy costs.

Following their recent and misguided increase in corporation tax, the Conservatives can no longer be viewed as a party of low taxes. In other words, higher-rate tax relief is not safe in their hands.

Furthermore, pensions are long-term savings vehicles, with contributions often made over many decades. It would be very brave to predict that the same level of tax relief will be available in five, 10 or 20 years' time.

If there is a further raid on pension tax relief it could come in the form of a further reduction in the annual allowance (from, say, £40,000 to £30,000 or £20,000) or a flat-rate model could be introduced with everyone given tax relief at say 25% or 30%. Another more radical option would be to completely replace the current pension model with something similar to the Lifetime ISA (see Chapter 14 for more on Lifetime ISAs).

The truth is nobody knows what will happen to pension tax relief in the years ahead, although further changes do seem likely at some point.

For several years now pension companies have advised higher-rate taxpayers to make bigger pension contributions before the extra tax relief is scrapped. To date all such predictions have been proved wrong. Nevertheless it is a concern that the pension tax reliefs seem to be continually on the Government's radar.

Many higher-rate taxpayers may feel they have nothing to lose by making bigger contributions with full 40% tax relief while this is still possible.

The ongoing saga around pension tax relief highlights the major drawback of this savings vehicle: almost every benefit can be taken away by politicians at the stroke of a pen.

They can change the tax reliefs, the age you can access your savings, restrict how you invest your savings and make withdrawals and increase the tax paid on the money you take out or leave to your family.

Most changes in recent years have definitely been for the better; future ones could be for the worse – politicians love to make gifts and then take them back!

Part 2

Taking Money Out: The Pension Freedom Rules

Chapter 7

Introduction

Before Age 55

At present you cannot withdraw any money from your pension until you're 55. This is one of the major drawbacks. There are times in life when even financially conservative individuals may need to tap their retirement savings early.

Obvious examples would be to pay for a child's education or unforeseen family medical expenses. In the worst case scenario you may even need to access your savings early to avoid bankruptcy or home repossession. So if you're under 55 and want to make significant pension contributions you should make sure you have other resources to protect against:

- Unforeseen expenses, and an
- Unforeseen drop in income.

Although you cannot withdraw anything until you're 55, it's important to point out that the money can usually be invested as you please. These days many personal pensions plans, especially SIPPs, provide enormous investment flexibility.

Note too that 55 is the minimum age set out in the legislation. The rules of a particular workplace pension scheme may impose a higher minimum age for payment of scheme benefits.

The Ill Health Exceptions

There are mainly two exceptions to the no withdrawals before age 55 rule. All pension savings can be withdrawn as a lump sum if you suffer from "serious ill health" (the polite way of saying you have less than a year to live). Withdrawals are tax free before age 75, taxable if 75 or older. You may also be able to start withdrawing money from your pension if you suffer from "ill health". This means you are not about to die but are too sick to carry on your current occupation (some scheme rules may state that you have to be incapable of carrying on *any* occupation).

Future Changes to the Minimum Pension Age

On 6th April 2028 the minimum age at which people can access their private pensions is expected to increase from 55 to 57, when the state pension age is increased to 67. So if you were born on or after 6th April 1973, you may have to wait at least another two years before you can tap your savings.

The increase in the minimum pension age from 55 to 57 has been put into legislation as part of the Finance Act 2022.

The increase will not apply to members of the armed forces, police and fire services who do not already have a protected pension age.

The legislation also introduces a "protected pension age". Members of registered pension schemes (occupational or non-occupational) who have an existing right under the scheme's rules to take pension benefits at age 55 will be protected from the increase to 57 in 2028.

The right to take benefits at 55 must have been in the scheme's rules as of 11th February 2021. New members of such schemes will also be protected as long as they joined before 4th November 2021.

Members of pension schemes who do not have such a right will see their minimum pension age increase to 57 on 6th April 2028.

Further Increases in the Pension Age

The Government's position is that it is, in principle, appropriate for the age at which people can access their private pensions to remain around 10 years below the state pension age. However, the Government has not created an automatic link yet.

The November 2022 Autumn Statement mentioned that: *"The State Pension age is legislated to increase over the next 25 years. There is currently a Review of the State Pension age being carried out which is considering whether the existing timetable remains appropriate. The Secretary of State for Work and Pensions will publish the government's Review of the State Pension age in early 2023. The Review will need to carefully balance important factors, including fiscal sustainability, the economic context, the latest life expectancy data and fairness both to pensioners and taxpayers."*

Pension Freedom

When you're 55 (or 57 from 2028) you can start tapping your pension. You can take out as much money as you like, whenever you like.

You can withdraw the whole lot in one go or leave your entire pension pot untouched and give it to your family when you die (see Chapter 10).

Most people will probably do something in between these two extremes. For example, when you're 55 or 57 you could take your tax-free lump sum and leave the rest of your savings to grow tax free until you retire and then start withdrawing income gradually.

Saving tax will be a key consideration (see Chapter 11).

Under the pension freedom rules you can use one or more of the following products to access your pension:

- Flexi-access drawdown
- Uncrystallised funds pension lump sum (UFPLS)
- Lifetime annuity

Flexi-access drawdown lets you take your entire tax-free lump sum in one go and place your remaining savings into drawdown, where the money can be accessed as and when you like.

Taking an uncrystallised funds pension lump sum allows you to take your tax-free lump sum in stages instead of in one go. Like drawdown, you can make withdrawals as and when you like but one quarter of every withdrawal will be tax free with the remainder taxed as income.

Annuities have been unpopular in recent years because they've been paying out paltry amounts of income (when interest rates were very so low). However, there are reports that they're coming back into fashion now that interest rates have increased. They've also been unpopular because the life insurance company generally confiscates your pension savings when you die or your spouse dies. Despite their drawbacks, annuities do provide a guaranteed "risk-free" income for life, unlike drawdown and UFPLS.

The various income options are discussed further in Chapter 8.

Final Salary Pensions

The pension freedom reforms apply to "defined contribution" pensions only: personal pensions and SIPPs and many occupational pension schemes in the private sector.

They're not available to members of final salary pension schemes (also known as defined benefit schemes). Members of these schemes cannot withdraw money as and when they like.

However, if you belong to a final salary scheme it may be possible to transfer to a defined contribution scheme (such as a SIPP) and collect a large cash lump sum. The value of final salary transfers often runs to hundreds of thousands of pounds.

Members of unfunded public sector pension schemes (i.e. teachers, NHS employees and civil servants) are not able to transfer to a defined contribution scheme and access their pension as a lump sum. Unfunded pension schemes are ones that don't have any assets – they rely on taxpayers to keep up the pension payments.

Members of funded public sector schemes (such as the local government pension scheme) are able to transfer to a defined contribution scheme.

Transferring to a personal pension may allow you to access your pension savings more flexibly and leave surplus funds to your children.

However, pension transfers are also highly controversial, which is why impartial professional advice is necessary.

Many pension experts advise against transferring from a "gold-plated" final salary scheme, which offers a guaranteed income for life, to a "crummy" personal pension, where your retirement income will depend on how well your investments perform. Members of final salary schemes do not have to worry about the ups and downs of the stock market!

Research by pension consultancy XPS has also shown that people who transfer out of final salary schemes are paying record annual fees in their new schemes (1.9% per year on average). The difference between the cheapest and most expensive pension schemes amounts to an additional £8,500 per year in charges.

Tax on Pension Withdrawals

Although you can take one quarter of your pension savings as a tax-free lump sum, you have to pay income tax on everything else you withdraw, *including your original contributions*.

That's a bit like putting £100 in a bank account and paying £20 or maybe £40 tax when you withdraw the money a year later. Of course, this doesn't happen when you withdraw money from your bank account – at most you will pay tax on your interest.

So while pensions offer several tax concessions, there is a tax sting at the end.

Thus, the sixty-four-thousand dollar question is this:

Do the tax benefits – tax relief on contributions and tax-free investment growth – outweigh the penalty of taxed withdrawals?

In most cases the answer is "Yes". This is because most people will probably pay basic-rate tax (currently 20%) on the money they take out but will enjoy 40% tax relief when they put their money in, if they are higher-rate taxpayers.

Furthermore, some of the money you take out will be tax free, including your tax-free lump sum and any withdrawals that are covered by your income tax personal allowance.

This is why even basic-rate taxpayers will usually also end up better off with a pension. Although they only enjoy basic-rate tax relief when they put their money in, a significant chunk of the money they take out could be tax free.

But *exactly* how much better off are you likely to be with a pension? The benefits surely have to be significant to justify putting your money into a locked box until you are 55 or older.

One way to answer this question is to compare two investors: one putting money into a pension and the other putting money into a different tax shelter, an ISA, and see who ends up better off at the end of the day. We do this in Chapter 15.

Like pensions, money in ISAs grows tax free. However, unlike pensions, ISAs do not offer any upfront tax relief but all your withdrawals are tax free and your money is not tied up until age 55 or later – you can withdraw it whenever you like.

However, the problem with using ISAs as retirement saving vehicles is they give you tax relief when you may need it least. It's usually better to have 40% tax relief when you put your money in, as you do with pensions if you're a higher-rate taxpayer, rather than 20% tax relief when you take it out, as you would with ISAs (most individuals are basic-rate taxpayers when they retire).

If you're under 40 you can also invest in a Lifetime ISA. These arguably offer the best of both worlds: upfront tax relief (in the shape of a Government bonus) and tax-free withdrawals. We also compare Lifetime ISAs and pensions in Chapter 15.

Pension Advice

The Pensions Advice Allowance allows you to withdraw £500 tax free from your pension pot on three occasions (i.e. three separate tax years) to pay for pensions and retirement advice. The allowance is available at any age and to members of defined contribution pension schemes (not final salary pension schemes). Not all pension providers offer this facility, however.

Chapter 8

Flexi-Access Drawdown & UFPLS

If you want to make use of the flexible regime for pension withdrawals you have two choices:

- Flexi-access drawdown
- Uncrystallised funds pension lump sum (UFPLS)

Some pension providers will only offer very limited options so you may have to shop around and, in some cases, it may even be necessary to transfer your pension to another provider.

Flexi-Access Drawdown

When you reach pension age (currently 55) you can move some or all of your pension savings into flexi-access drawdown.

One quarter (25%) can be taken as a tax-free cash lump sum and only flexi-access drawdown allows you to take your tax-free lump sum on its own without any additional taxable income (for example, if you want to withdraw some cash to pay down your mortgage before you stop working).

The remaining 75% continues to grow tax free in your drawdown fund until you withdraw it. You can withdraw as much income as you like whenever you like. All withdrawals will be fully taxed.

If at any point you decide you want a more secure income for the rest of your life, you can use some or all of your remaining drawdown funds to buy an annuity.

Phased Drawdown

If you don't want to take your entire tax-free lump sum in one go, you can use something called phased drawdown. For example, you may wish to withdraw a small tax-free lump sum to reduce your mortgage or for home improvements.

Phased drawdown may also appeal to those who are semi-retired. It allows you to make regular tax-free withdrawals to supplement your income before you are fully retired.

Then when you stop working completely (and your tax rate is hopefully lower) you can start withdrawing money from the taxable portion of your pension pot.

By not withdrawing your entire lump sum in one go it can continue to grow tax free inside your pension. As a result you may end up with more tax-free cash overall.

Example
Stacey is 58 and still working and has a pension pot worth £200,000. She wants to take just £10,000 out of her pension tax free. She transfers £40,000 into a flexi-access drawdown plan and takes the 25% tax-free lump sum of £10,000 and leaves the remaining £30,000 in the drawdown plan without taking any additional taxable income.

A couple of years later she transfers another £40,000 into the drawdown plan and takes another £10,000 of tax-free cash. She leaves the remaining £30,000 in the drawdown plan, along with the other £30,000 from two years ago.

She can keep doing this until she has transferred all of her pension pot into flexi-access drawdown.

Uncrystallised Funds Pension Lump Sum (UFPLS)

The pension freedom reforms were clearly made in a hurry. How else can you explain calling something an "uncrystallised funds pension lump sum", with the unwieldy acronym UFPLS?

With UFPLS you can take your entire pension pot as a lump sum in one go, or take a series of smaller lump sums. Each lump sum will have a 25% tax-free element, with the rest taxed as income.

UFPLS may appeal to those who don't need all their tax-free cash immediately. Instead it can continue to grow tax free. Note, however, that a similar result can be achieved with flexi-access drawdown by using phased drawdown (if your pension provider offers it) and crystallising just a portion of your retirement savings.

Example

Zach has a £100,000 pension pot. He withdraws £20,000 using UFPLS, leaving £80,000 untouched. £5,000 of the UFPLS is tax-free cash, the remaining £15,000 is taxable. If we assume Zach has other income and is a basic-rate taxpayer he will pay 20% tax: £3,000. Zach can continue to use UFPLS to take lump sums as and when he needs. He can also move his remaining pension pot into flexi-access drawdown or, if he wants a secure income for the rest of his life with no investment risk, he can use his remaining funds to buy an annuity.

With UFPLS you have to take tax-free cash and taxable income at the same time – every withdrawal will consist of 25% tax-free cash and 75% taxable income.

Flexi-access drawdown is therefore more flexible because it lets you take tax-free cash without having to take any taxable income. This may be more appealing if you want to withdraw cash while you are still working and paying 40% tax. You can postpone withdrawing taxable income until you retire and start paying tax at 20% (at present most retirees are basic-rate taxpayers).

The Money Purchase Annual Allowance (MPAA)

When you start withdrawing money from your pension pot you can continue making pension contributions but you may be subject to the money purchase annual allowance (MPAA).

The money purchase annual allowance used to be £10,000 but was reduced to £4,000 a number of years back.

Being limited to an annual pension contribution of just £4,000 (compared with the normal £40,000 annual allowance) makes it very difficult for those who have accessed their pension savings (perhaps through financial hardship) to rebuild them.

If you are subject to the money purchase annual allowance you also cannot carry forward any unused allowance from previous tax years.

Note that £4,000 is the maximum *gross* pension contribution you could make. The maximum cash you could invest personally would be £3,200. The taxman would add £800 of basic-rate tax relief to produce a gross pension contribution of £4,000.

If you use flexi-access drawdown and take your 25% tax-free lump but do not withdraw any additional taxable income, you get to keep your £40,000 annual allowance, i.e. you can keep making pension contributions just like anyone else.

However, as soon as you take any income from your drawdown fund the money purchase annual allowance will apply.

With uncrystallised funds pension lump sums (UFPLS) the money purchase annual allowance applies once you start making any pension withdrawals. In other words, as soon as you start withdrawing money using UFPLS your pension contributions could be restricted to £4,000 per year.

Thus, flexi-access drawdown may be more suitable for those who want to keep making pension contributions. You can withdraw some or all of your tax-free cash and keep making pension contributions of up to £40,000 per year and use your unused annual allowance from the previous three tax years.

The money purchase annual allowance was introduced to reduce pension recycling – taking income out of a pension and using it to make fresh contributions with tax relief.

It is also designed to prevent those aged 55 and over replacing their regular taxed salaries with employer pension contributions, 25% of which could be withdrawn tax free immediately.

Note that additional rules prevent tax-free lump sums being recycled (see Chapter 9).

The MPAA only applies to money purchase pension contributions (e.g. those paid into personal pensions and SIPPs). It does not restrict contributions to defined benefit pension schemes (final salary schemes).

In other words, your annual allowance for funding a final salary scheme will generally still be £40,000, less any money purchase contributions within the £4,000 limit.

The money purchase annual allowance also isn't triggered if:

- You use your pension savings to buy a standard lifetime annuity

- You are using capped drawdown (the old type of drawdown that is no longer available to new retirees) and do not withdraw income above the maximum income limit

- You cash in a small pension pot. You can take up to three pension pots worth up to £10,000 each (an unlimited number from occupational pension schemes)

PAYE Issues

When you withdraw income from your pension, the pension provider will deduct income tax before paying you.

If your pension provider does not hold a current P45 form for you (usually only issued when you stop working), tax will be deducted at the so-called emergency rate. In many cases this will mean that far too much tax is deducted and you will be due a refund.

For example, if you withdraw £10,000 from your pension at the start of the tax year you could be taxed as if your total income is £120,000 for the year.

The refund can be claimed at the end of the tax year or you can claim the tax back during the year (apparently within 30 days).

If you decide to make a single withdrawal that does not empty your pension pot, you can claim back the tax overpaid by completing a P55 form.

Those intending to make a series of irregular withdrawals are advised to talk to their pension providers. After applying emergency tax to the first payment, the pension provider might be able to report a zero payment for the months where no withdrawal is made and correct the tax deducted on subsequent withdrawals.

Another form P50Z is to be used if you empty your entire pension pot in a single withdrawal and have no other PAYE or pension income (other than your state pension). Form P53Z should be used if you have other employment income or pensions.

Chapter 9

The Pension Recycling Rules

When you start withdrawing income from a flexi-access drawdown plan or make any withdrawal using UFPLS, you will be subject to the money purchase annual allowance.

This may limit your future money purchase pension contributions to £4,000 per year and prohibit you from carrying forward any unused annual allowance from previous tax years.

If you use flexi-access drawdown and withdraw your tax-free lump sum only (with no additional income) you can continue making pension contributions of up to £40,000 per year (if you have sufficient earnings) and use any unused annual allowance from the previous three tax years.

However, if you use your tax-free lump sum to make new pension contributions, you have to be wary of HMRC's recycling rules. These are designed to prevent tax-free cash being reinvested in a pension and enjoying a second round of tax relief.

Example
Toby is 59, still working and a higher-rate taxpayer. Over the last 10 years he has been making pension contributions of £6,000 per year. Using flexi-access drawdown he withdraws £10,000 of tax-free cash in order to reinvest it in a pension. The taxman adds £2,500 of basic-rate tax relief, giving him a total gross pension contribution of £12,500. Furthermore, when he submits his tax return he receives higher-rate tax relief of £2,500.

Unfortunately for Toby his pension contribution may fall foul of HMRC's recycling rules which are designed to prevent you making larger than normal pension contributions because you have received a tax-free lump sum.

The recycling rules can even apply if you make bigger than normal pension contributions *before* you withdraw tax-free cash.

If the recycling rules apply, your tax-free lump sum will be treated as an unauthorised payment, resulting in a tax charge of up to 70%.

The recycling rules apply when ALL of the following conditions are met:

- You receive a pension commencement lump sum (tax-free lump sum)

- The tax-free cash, including any tax-free cash taken in the previous 12 months, exceeds £7,500

- Because you took tax-free cash your pension contributions are significantly larger than they otherwise would be

- The additional contributions are more than 30% of the tax-free cash

- The recycling was pre-planned

Point 2 means that small amounts of recycling effectively fall under the radar.

Example
Using phased drawdown Justine takes a tax-free lump sum of £7,000 and immediately invests all of it in a pension plan, producing a gross pension contribution of £8,750 after basic-rate tax relief is added. She hasn't received any other tax-free cash in the previous 12 months so the pension contribution does not fall foul of the recycling rules, even though the recycling was pre-planned.

Looking at point 3, for the recycling rules to apply there must be a significant increase in your pension contributions. This includes contributions made by you and your employer.

HMRC will look at your contribution history to determine if there has been a significant increase. If you haven't made any pension contributions for a while, your last contribution may be adjusted for inflation to produce a current value for comparison purposes.

As a rule of thumb, HMRC may argue that your pension contributions have increased significantly if they are 30% larger than they would have been without the tax-free cash.

HMRC doesn't just look for big pension contributions in the tax year you receive tax-free cash. They will also look at contributions made in the two tax years before you received the cash and in the two tax years after you took the cash.

Example
Harvey is 60 and for the last five years has been making pension contributions of £10,000 per year. He takes a £40,000 tax-free lump sum from his pension and uses some of it to pay for a new kitchen and the rest to make a £25,000 pension contribution in the next tax year. Because his pension contribution is more than 30% larger than those made in recent years he may fall foul of the pension recycling rules.

The amount of additional contributions is measured on a cumulative basis which means you may be caught out even if you only make relatively small additional pension contributions after receiving your tax-free cash.

Example
Joan has been making pension contributions of £10,000 per year for the last 10 years. She takes £20,000 of tax-free cash from her pension and uses some of it to increase her pension contributions as follows:

	Contribution	*Increase*	*% Increase*
Current year	£12,500	£2,500	25%
One year later	£12,500	£2,500	25%
Two years later	£12,500	£2,500	25%
Cumulative increase		£7,500	75%

Joan's pension contributions have not increased by more than 30% in any single year but the cumulative increase is 75%. This is more than 30% which means there has been a significant increase.

Because the additional pension contributions were pre-planned she may have to pay £14,000 tax on the £20,000 tax-free lump sum.

Turning to point 4, you'll only be caught by the recycling rules if your additional contributions are more than 30% of your tax-free lump sum. In Joan's case her additional contributions were £7,500 and are more than 30% of her tax-free lump sum (£20,000 x 30% = £6,000).

However, if her additional contributions were less than £2,000 per year (less than £6,000 in total) this would presumably not count as pension recycling.

Point 5 is the most vague. The recycling must be pre-planned which means you must have intended to take your tax-free lump sum to make significantly greater pension contributions.

If you decide to use your tax-free lump sum to significantly increase your pension contributions but make the contributions *before* receiving your tax-free lump sum this will also be treated as pre-planning (for example, if you use other savings or a loan to pay the contributions and then use your lump sum to replenish those savings or pay off the loan).

Where, on the other hand, you take a lump sum and only later decide to use it to make bigger contributions, there is no pre-planning.

When the Recycling Rules Do Not Apply

The key is that the recycling rules only apply when your pension contributions are significantly increased "because of" the tax-free lump sum.

There are other reasons why your pension contributions may increase significantly from year to year and they will not constitute recycling.

For example, let's say you increase your pension contributions from £10,000 to £15,000 in the year you take tax-free cash. Although your pension contributions have increased by more than 30% this may be because you've received a bonus or the profits of your business have increased or because you have more income taxed at 40% and want to maximise your higher-rate tax relief.

As long as you can demonstrate that, although your pension contributions have fluctuated, they are calculated on a consistent basis (e.g. as a percentage of your income) the recycling rules should not apply.

The recycling rules will also not apply if you make significantly larger pension contributions because you receive a cash windfall such as an inheritance.

Example
Sadie takes tax-free cash from her pension. A few months later her father dies leaving her a substantial inheritance. Because of the inheritance (and not because she received a pension lump sum), she decides to make larger than normal pension contributions. She invests the whole inheritance in her pension. These pension contributions will not constitute recycling because she did not pre-plan to use the pension lump sum to make significantly larger pension contributions.

In summary, it is probably possible to trickle some of your tax-free lump sum back into a pension, providing the additional annual contributions are very small and made over many tax years.

However, it's important to stress that this is high-risk tax planning because if you get it wrong the penalties are severe.

Anyone thinking of making larger than normal pension contributions a couple of years before or after taking tax-free cash should probably seek professional advice.

Chapter 10

Leaving Your Pension Pot to Your Family

Pensions have become a lot more attractive when it comes to leaving money to your family.

After you die your pension pot can be transferred tax free to any member of your family (or anyone else for that matter).

The new rules have applied since 6th April 2015.

Under the old rules, a 55% "death tax" was generally payable, leaving just 45% for your family.

The 55% tax could be avoided by using your pension savings to provide a "dependant's pension" for your spouse or children under 23. Of course, most people die when their children are over 23, so it usually wasn't possible to leave pension savings to children without paying the death tax.

The rules were more generous if you died before age 75 – your entire pension pot could be paid out tax free to your family... but only if you hadn't started withdrawing money.

The Current Rules

Death before Age 75

Your pension savings can be paid tax free to any beneficiary. It doesn't matter whether you've started withdrawing money or not.

Your beneficiaries can take the money as a tax-free lump sum or keep the money invested in a drawdown plan and make tax free withdrawals as and when they like – they don't have to wait until reaching the minimum pension age (currently 55).

The drawdown investments will continue to grow tax free until income is withdrawn.

Lump sum death benefits are only tax free if paid out within two years of the pension scheme administrator becoming aware of the member's death. Similarly, where uncrystallised pension savings are placed into flexi-access drawdown, withdrawals will only be tax-free if the drawdown designation is made within two years.

75 or Older

The 55% death tax has been abolished which means your beneficiaries can inherit all of your pension savings.

They will still have to pay income tax on any money they withdraw, just like you would, but they can also keep the money invested where it will continue to grow tax free for as long as they like, perhaps until they themselves retire.

There are no restrictions on the amount of income they can withdraw, i.e. the whole pension pot can be paid out in a single tax year, although this may not be very tax efficient.

Example
Helen dies aged 80, leaving pension savings of £100,000. Her son Kevin is her nominated beneficiary. He earns a salary of £60,000 per year. Helen's pension savings are placed into a drawdown plan for Kevin and he withdraws all the money as income during the current tax year.

Kevin will end up paying additional tax of £45,528 on the pension withdrawal. This is because his income for the year is now £160,000 which means he loses his income tax personal allowance and pays 45% tax on some of the pension withdrawal.

It may be more tax efficient for Kevin to leave the money growing tax free in the drawdown plan until he himself retires and then start making gradual withdrawals which will probably be taxed at the basic rate of income tax (currently 20%).

Inheritance Tax

It's important to point out that your pension savings are typically held in trust outside your estate and are thus free from inheritance tax in most cases.

This is because the administrator of the pension scheme normally has discretion over who gets the money, although they will typically be guided by your wishes, which can be stated by completing a simple expression of wishes form.

Because these forms are usually not legally binding (although rarely ignored), your pension savings will not form part of your estate for inheritance tax purposes.

Note, not all pension monies will escape inheritance tax. For example, an inheritance tax charge may arise if you make unusually large pension contributions because you are in ill health and then die within two years. (An individual may do this to try to take some of their assets out of the inheritance tax net.)

Note, if you make pension contributions while you are in normal health there will be no inheritance tax consequences.

Where contributions are made more than two years before death HMRC will assume that you were in normal health, unless there is evidence to the contrary.

An inheritance tax charge may also arise if you transfer from one pension scheme to another while in ill health and die within two years of making the transfer.

The intention of the person making the transfer is crucial. For example, if the transfer was made solely to benefit someone else (e.g. your children) inheritance tax may be payable. An example would be a transfer out of a final salary scheme, with limited death benefits, to a personal pension, which offers more flexibility.

If the transfer is made from one defined contribution scheme to another and the transfer was made for genuine commercial reasons, for example to benefit from lower charges, the transfer should be exempt from inheritance tax.

It's a grey area and professional advice is recommended.

Nest & Inheritance Tax

Nest is the pension scheme set up by the Government to handle auto-enrolment. It has over eight million members.

Death benefits paid from Nest used to always form part of the member's estate for inheritance tax purposes. This was because members could only nominate a beneficiary, with no discretion. Nest members can still nominate a beneficiary and this means the retirement pot will be paid to the person nominated and will usually form part of the estate for inheritance tax purposes.

Nest members can now also make an expression of wish which means that their wish and current circumstances will be considered when Nest decides who the money goes to. As a result, the pension pot won't usually be subject to inheritance tax.

Tax Planning

With the 55% death tax abolished, combined with an exemption from inheritance tax in most cases, pensions are powerful vehicles for passing wealth tax free from one generation to another.

The assets in the plan will continue to grow tax free and the only tax payable by your beneficiaries will be income tax on withdrawals. They won't pay any income tax on their withdrawals if you die before age 75.

Your nominated beneficiaries (e.g. your children) can then pass on any unused funds to their own nominated beneficiaries (e.g. your grandchildren) and so on.

The grandchildren will pay tax on their withdrawals if your children die after reaching age 75. No tax will be payable if your children die before age 75.

Preserving Your Pension Pot

Because pension pots are potentially useful inheritance tax shelters, some advisers recommend that wealthy retirees who are worried about inheritance tax should consider using up their other assets before withdrawing income from their pensions.

For example, after you have withdrawn your tax-free lump sum you could place the rest of your pension savings in a drawdown plan and leave most of it growing tax free for your family. You could then use your other assets to fund your retirement, e.g. rental properties and ISAs.

Of course, most retirees cannot afford to leave all their pension savings intact. But most will have at least some pension savings left to pass on to family members.

So for almost everyone it is good news that the 55% death tax has been abolished. It put some people off making significant pension contributions and put some retirees under pressure to withdraw income from their pensions as quickly as possible, with potentially adverse income tax consequences.

Minimising Tax on Withdrawals

Parents who wish to pass on their pension pots to their children may need to teach them how to withdraw money tax efficiently. For a pension to be an effective inter-generational tax shelter it's important your beneficiaries' withdrawals are taxed at the basic rate of income tax (currently 20%) or less.

This isn't a problem if you die before age 75 because your beneficiaries (e.g. your children) will be able to withdraw the money tax free. However, there are still things they can do to produce a better financial outcome.

For example, if your children aren't worried about their own inheritance tax it may be more tax efficient for them to withdraw all the money tax free rather than pass on the pension pot to your grandchildren, who will have to pay income tax on their own withdrawals (if your children die after reaching age 75).

Your beneficiaries could also withdraw money from your pension pot to fund pension contributions of their own. With higher-rate tax relief this could leave them significantly better off overall.

If you die after reaching age 75 the withdrawals made by your beneficiaries will be taxed. However, tax-free withdrawals can be made if your beneficiaries have no other income and the withdrawals are covered by their income tax personal allowance (currently £12,570). This may be the case if they are at university, starting a business or taking time off work to raise children.

Pension withdrawals taxed at the basic rate can be made by your beneficiaries as long as these withdrawals do not take them over the higher-rate threshold – currently £50,270 (£43,662 in Scotland).

Example

Andrew, age 74, dies with £200,000 left in his pension plan. His wife Diane, age 70, is his beneficiary. She decides to keep the money in a drawdown plan so that it can continue to grow tax free and remains outside her estate for inheritance tax purposes. She withdraws a tax-free income of around £15,000 per year until she dies aged 80. At this point there is £150,000 left in the drawdown fund.

Until recently Diane's daughter Brenda was her nominated beneficiary. Brenda is a successful GP and a higher-rate taxpayer. If she inherits the pension pot she will pay 40% tax on any withdrawals.

So a few years ago Brenda encouraged Diane to nominate her two grandchildren as beneficiaries. They are currently aged 18 and 20 and at university. Thanks to Brenda's forward thinking, the grandchildren can withdraw tax-free income each year to use up their income tax personal allowances and help them through university. Then when they start working they can continue withdrawing money and may only pay tax at 20% if they are basic-rate taxpayers. Alternatively they can keep the remaining savings invested tax free until they need it, possibly when they themselves retire if they are extremely prudent!

Nominating Beneficiaries

It's important to make sure your pension provider has an up to date expression of wishes form which is simple to complete and is used to nominate who should receive your pension savings when you die. The form can be used to nominate more than one person.

Chapter 11

How to Save Tax When You Tap Your Pension

When the pension withdrawal rules were relaxed there were fears that retirees would blow their pensions on expensive holidays and Lamborghinis. A few reckless individuals will no doubt squander their savings but the vast majority will probably withdraw the money gradually and spend it wisely.

Nevertheless, there is still a danger that even careful retirees will spend their savings a bit too quickly and end up depleting their pension pots.

Those who want a guaranteed income for life, with no danger of running out of money, can always hand over their retirement savings to an annuity provider. For example, a 65 year old with a £200,000 pension pot can currently buy a guaranteed income for life of around £7,000 per year and possibly more. This will increase with inflation and continue providing a pension for their widow.

This is significantly higher than in previous years because annuity rates have risen in line with interest rates.

It may be possible to achieve a higher income by using a drawdown arrangement and investing in, for example, companies with a long track record of paying growing dividends, or other investments. However, your income will not be guaranteed and could fall, as could the value of your investments.

This is the dilemma retirees face in the wake of George Osborne's pension revolution. Freedom to spend your pension savings as you like does not necessarily buy you peace of mind.

You should probably only spend a tiny fraction of your pension savings each year if they are to last through your retirement. Some retirees may, however, wish to make bigger than normal withdrawals and this doesn't necessarily mean they're going to fritter the money away.

For example, you could make bigger than normal withdrawals to:

- Invest in tax-free ISAs
- Buy rental property
- Reduce mortgages or other debts
- Start a business

One thing retirees no longer have to do is make bigger than normal pension withdrawals to avoid the 55% death tax (see Chapter 10). If anything, surplus money should remain invested in your pension pot for as long as possible so that it can be passed on to your family free from inheritance tax.

Tax will be an extremely important factor when it comes to deciding how much you withdraw from your pension and when. In this chapter we're going to take a closer look at some of the strategies pension savers may be able to follow to pay less income tax and capital gains tax.

These days retirees have the freedom to control their tax bills to some extent by making bigger pension withdrawals in some tax years and smaller withdrawals in other years.

Saving Income Tax

Any money you withdraw from your pension, over and above your 25% tax-free lump sum, is subject to income tax. If you withdraw a lot in one go you could end up paying tax at 40% or even 45%.

Most retirees should endeavour to pay no more than basic-rate tax on their pension withdrawals (currently 20%). One way to achieve this is by spreading withdrawals over many tax years.

During the current 2022/23 tax year (and through to the end of the 2027/28 tax year) you will pay no more than basic-rate tax if your taxable income from all sources is less than £50,270. At present most retirees do not earn more than £50,270 per year and should therefore refrain from making big pension withdrawals that push them into the 40% tax bracket.

In Scotland the higher-rate threshold is currently £43,662. At this income level the tax rate increases from 21% to 41%.

Example

It's the start of the 2022/23 tax year. Andrew is 60 and earns a salary of £60,000. He has been saving into a pension and ISA. His pension pot is worth £200,000 and his ISA savings are worth £100,000. His wife Elizabeth is the same age and has similar income and savings.

If for whatever reason Andrew decided to withdraw all of his pension savings in one go, one quarter (£50,000) would be tax free. The remaining £150,000 would be fully taxed. His total taxable income would be £210,000 (£60,000 salary plus £150,000 pension).

With this much income, all of his pension income would be taxed at either 40% or 45% and he would lose his income tax personal allowance.

Andrew's total income tax bill would rise from £11,432 (salary only) to £79,460. He would end up paying tax at an effective rate of 45.35% on his pension withdrawal.

Furthermore, the money he takes out would no longer grow tax free outside his pension plan.

Fortunately, Andrew has no need to tap his pension pot at this time and realizes he is better off leaving the money alone while he is working full time.

He doesn't even want to withdraw his tax-free lump sum because he has no use for it at present and wants it to continue growing tax free.

In fact, instead of taking money out, he intends to keep putting money into both his pension and ISA. He enjoys higher-rate tax relief on his pension contributions.

This is one of the reasons why pension savers need to be careful about tapping their savings too early. If you are using flexi-access drawdown and withdraw any income over and above your tax-free lump sum, your future pension contributions could be limited to just £4,000 per year (see Chapter 8).

A similar restriction applies if you withdraw any money as an uncrystallised funds pension lump sum (UFPLS).

Example continued

Three years later it's 2025/26 and Andrew is 63. He decides to resign from his job because he wants to work part time. His pension pot is now worth £270,000 and his ISA savings are worth £175,000. Before getting a part-time job he decides to take a year off to pursue various interests, including buying and renovating a rental property. Andrew and Elizabeth withdraw their 25% tax-free lump sums to purchase the property (£135,000 in total) and put the rest of their pension savings into drawdown plans.

Although the property will eventually produce <u>taxable</u> income and capital gains (whereas the money was growing tax free inside their pensions), Andrew and Elizabeth believe they have found a genuine bargain which makes up for the loss of tax relief.

Because he has no other taxable income at present, Andrew withdraws an additional £12,570 tax free from his pension to avoid wasting his personal allowance. He could also withdraw an extra £37,700 taxed at just 20%.

Because he has withdrawn <u>income</u> from his pension, his future pension contributions will be limited to £4,000 per year. This does not cause Andrew any problems.

Example continued

A year later Andrew is 64 and gets a part-time job earning £15,000. He also earns £5,000 rent from his share of the property. If he doesn't need more income he can leave his pension pot to grow tax free. If he wants more income he can take another £30,000 taxed at just 20%.

Two years later Andrew is 66 and has reached state pension age and decides to stop working. His pension pot is now worth around £230,000 and his ISA savings have grown to over £200,000. Coupled with Elizabeth's savings and the income from the rental property, he feels financially secure enough to retire.

His state pension and rental income use up his income tax personal allowance so he will pay at least 20% tax on any income he withdraws from his pension in future. Keeping an eye on how his drawdown investments are performing, he varies the amount he withdraws each year but makes sure he never pays 40% income tax.

Reducing Capital Gains Tax

Because retirees can choose how much money they withdraw from their pension pots each year, they can halt or reduce withdrawals in years they sell assets like rental property and reduce their capital gains tax bills.

This is because you only pay 18% capital gains tax (as opposed to 28%) to the extent your basic-rate band is not used up by your income*. For example, at present if you don't have any taxable income you can have £37,700 of capital gains taxed at 18%.

The potential tax saving is £7,540 per couple:

$$£37,700 \times 2 \times 10\% = £7,540$$

* Note these are the capital gains tax rates for residential property. The rates for other assets are 10% and 20% respectively.

Example continued

Several years later Andrew and Elizabeth decide to sell their rental property because it has increased in value significantly and they don't want the hassle of managing tenants etc. They intend to use the proceeds to buy a holiday cottage.

After deducting various buying and selling costs and their annual CGT exemptions they expect to be left with taxable capital gains of £30,000 each. These amounts will be taxed at just 18%, providing they haven't withdrawn too much income from their pension pots.

(Note, the annual CGT exemption will be reduced from £12,300 to £6,000 from 6th April 2023 and to £3,000 from 6th April 2024.)

In the tax year before the sale takes place they therefore decide to make larger than normal pension withdrawals, but making sure they stay below the higher-rate threshold to avoid paying 40% tax.

In the tax year in which the property is sold they reduce their pension withdrawals so that all of their capital gains are taxed at 18%. They live off the extra income they withdrew during the previous tax year.

Once the sale has taken place, and they know how much of their basic-rate bands are left, they can withdraw some additional money from their pension pots taxed at just 20%.

Leaving Pension Wealth to Your Family

When you die your remaining pension savings can be left to your family (e.g. your spouse or children) who can keep the money growing tax free and make withdrawals as and when they like. The withdrawals will be subject to income tax if you die after reaching age 75.

ISA savings can also be left to family members but only your spouse can effectively keep them in the ISA tax wrapper (see Chapter 16).

Example continued
When Andrew dies at age 85 his remaining pension savings are left to Elizabeth. She also inherits his remaining ISA savings and is allowed to invest them in her own ISA.

Elizabeth now has two pension pots: her own and Andrew's. She wants to leave as much money as possible to her two children but she doesn't have to withdraw all her pension savings to avoid the now abolished 55% death tax.

Her remaining ISA savings can also be left to her children when she dies but the money will no longer be in a tax-free ISA and may be subject to inheritance tax.

One option would be to leave most of her pension savings intact and make tax-free withdrawals from her ISA to fund her living costs. This will reduce her estate for inheritance tax purposes.

If the children are likely to pay 40% income tax when they eventually inherit her pension savings, she could continue withdrawing income taxed at 20% in her hands and gift it to her children, although there may be inheritance tax consequences if she dies within seven years.

See the Taxcafe guide *How to Save Inheritance Tax* for more information about the various inheritance tax exemptions.

Withdrawing Lump Sums Gradually

Retirees who wish to make occasional large lump sum withdrawals should try to spread them over several tax years wherever possible.

Example
Barbara normally has income of £40,000, made up of rental income, her state pension and withdrawals from her personal pension. During the current tax year she wants to withdraw an additional £20,000 to pay for a log cabin garden office. If she withdraws all of the money during the current tax year, almost £10,000 will be taxed at 40%. If she withdraws the money over two tax years she will pay tax at 20%. Her total tax saving will be almost £2,000.

Big Contributions Close to Retirement

Because retirees can make unlimited pension withdrawals, it may be worth making bigger than normal pension contributions when you are close to retirement.

Example
Alan and Betty are both 60 and each earn £65,000 per year. At present, they make gross pension contributions of around £5,000 per year each. Betty's mother recently passed away, leaving her £70,000. Betty decides to give half the money to Alan so they can both ramp up their pension contributions before they stop working in five years' time. The reason Betty gives half the money to Alan and the couple spread their increased contributions over five tax years is so that higher-rate tax relief can be enjoyed on all of the additional contributions (see Chapter 4).

They're happy to make these increased pension contributions in the knowledge that the money will not be locked up because they have both reached the minimum pension age (although there are drawbacks to withdrawing pension income early – see Chapter 8).

They personally invest £35,000 each over a five year period, making sure they always enjoy full higher-rate tax relief on their additional contributions (see Chapter 4). For example, in 2022/23 they can make an additional gross pension contribution of up to £9,730 each:

£65,000 income - £50,270 higher-rate threshold - £5,000 existing contribution

This means a cash pension contribution of up to £7,784 (£9,730 x 0.8).

Over the five year period they invest £35,000 each and the taxman will add £8,750 basic-rate tax relief to each pension pot, so they end up with additional pension savings of £43,750 each. They also enjoy additional tax refunds of £8,750 each (their higher-rate tax relief).

Ignoring any tax-free investment growth they enjoy on these additional pension contributions, when they retire they'll each be able to withdraw an additional tax-free lump sum of £10,938 (£43,750 x 25%).

The remaining money (£32,812 each) will be fully taxed when withdrawn. If we assume the withdrawals are taxed at just 20%, Alan and Betty will each be left with £26,250. Depending on how much other income the couple have, these taxed withdrawals may have to be made over several tax years to avoid paying tax at 40%.

In total the couple receive higher-rate tax relief of £17,500, tax-free lump sums totalling £21,876 and after-tax income totalling £52,500. So their £70,000 investment has been transformed into £91,876.

The reason Alan and Betty did so well is they spread their pension contributions over more than one tax year to maximize higher-rate tax relief and spread their withdrawals over more than one tax year to minimise their income tax bills.

It may also be worth making bigger pension contributions close to retirement even if you only enjoy basic-rate tax relief... but the benefits are far smaller.

Example

Emily is 60 and intends to retire next year. In recent years she has been investing just enough in her pension to maximise her higher-rate tax relief (see Chapter 4). She has £24,000 in a savings account and decides to invest all of it in her pension. The taxman adds £6,000 of basic-rate tax relief so she ends up with additional pension savings of £30,000. There is no higher-rate tax relief on this additional contribution.

Soon after retiring she decides to withdraw the whole £30,000. One quarter (£7,500) will be tax free. Emily pays basic-rate tax at 20% on the remaining £22,500, leaving her £18,000. In total, Emily is left with £25,500, compared with her original investment of £24,000. She enjoys a £1,500 windfall from this simple piece of tax planning.

What the above examples reveal is that, where possible, pension contributions should always be spread over several tax years if this means more higher-rate tax relief can be enjoyed.

Big pension contributions that only result in basic-rate tax relief may still be worthwhile in some cases but the benefits are modest.

You also have to watch out for HMRC's recycling rules. These are designed to stop you taking a tax-free lump sum and reinvesting it in your pension with a second round of tax relief (see Chapter 9).

The recycling rules can also be triggered if you make big pension contributions in the two tax years *before* you start withdrawing money.

HMRC says that very few lump sums will be affected and the recycling rules are only triggered if you always intended your tax-free lump sum to be an integral part of paying for your increased contributions (either directly or indirectly).

Retirees with Other Income

Retirees who are currently basic-rate taxpayers but expect to become higher-rate taxpayers in the near future, may consider making bigger pension withdrawals now to avoid paying tax at 40% in future.

Why would you expect to become a higher-rate taxpayer? Perhaps if you expect to receive a windfall (for example, an inheritance) or because you expect your income to keep growing while the higher-rate threshold remains fixed at £50,270 until April 2028.

Example
Ann is 75 and widowed and has income of £30,000 from her state pension and some rental properties. She also has a personal pension pot worth £200,000 from which she withdraws roughly £10,000 per year. Her total income is £40,000 so she only pays 20% tax.

Her mother Betty is 95 and lives in a nursing home. Ann expects to inherit all of Betty's assets when she dies, giving her additional taxable income of roughly £25,000 per year. With this extra income Ann will become a higher-rate taxpayer and will effectively pay 40% tax on any income she withdraws from her pension.

Before Betty dies Ann decides to withdraw an additional £10,000 per year from her pension and invest the money in an ISA where it will continue to grow tax free. She reasons that it is better to pay an additional £2,000 per year income tax now rather than £4,000 per year at some point in the future as a higher-rate taxpayer.

Although Ann may save income tax by making bigger pension withdrawals before becoming a higher-rate taxpayer, she may end up aggravating a more significant long-term tax problem she faces – inheritance tax.

When Ann eventually dies, 40% inheritance tax could be payable on a significant chunk of her assets: her rental properties, the money she inherited from her mother and the additional money she withdrew from her pension and invested in an ISA.

She'll be able to leave her remaining pension savings to her children or grandchildren free from inheritance tax, although they will pay income tax on any money they withdraw, possibly at 40% or more.

Ann could therefore consider gifting the additional money she withdraws from her pension to her children or grandchildren rather than invest it in an ISA.

Alternatively, she could consider halting all withdrawals from her pension after she inherits her mother's assets. This will allow her to avoid paying income tax at 40% on her withdrawals and leave a bigger pension pot for her family to inherit.

Retirees with significant assets face a difficult juggling act deciding how much income to withdraw from their pensions to save both income tax and inheritance tax.

However, now that the 55% pension death tax has been scrapped they have considerably more flexibility and don't need to deplete their pension savings quickly.

Summary

- It is possible to make unlimited pension withdrawals when you reach pension age (55 rising to 57 in 2028).

- Any money you withdraw over and above your tax-free lump sum will be subject to income tax.

- At present, most retirees currently pay no more than 20% income tax and should avoid making withdrawals taxed at 40% or even 45%.

- This can be achieved by spreading withdrawals over many tax years, while keeping an eye on the £50,270 higher-rate threshold (£43,662 in Scotland).

- Taxable lump sum withdrawals should be spread over more than one tax year where practical.

- In most cases it will not be tax efficient to withdraw income if you are still working and a higher-rate taxpayer.

- In some cases it may be worth postponing pension withdrawals so that capital gains are taxed at 18% instead of 28%.

- Money left inside your pension pot when you die is generally not subject to inheritance tax.

- Your remaining pension savings can be left to anyone, for example your children or grandchildren. The money will continue to grow tax free but income tax will be paid on any withdrawals they make (unless you die before age 75).

Chapter 12

Pensions versus Buy-to-Let

Should you withdraw money from your pension to buy property?

This would only be worth considering if you think you can earn a better *after-tax* return from property than from your *tax-free* pension investments (typically shares and bonds).

Investing in property has become less attractive following two tax changes in recent years:

- 3% additional stamp duty land tax (4% in Scotland)
- Restricted tax relief on mortgage interest

Prior to April 2016 you wouldn't have paid any stamp duty land tax if you bought a rental property for £100,000... now you'll pay £3,000. You would have paid just £2,500 stamp duty if you bought a property for £250,000... at present you'll pay £7,500, rising to £10,000 after 31st March 2025.

When you add legal fees and mortgage arrangement fees, buying investment property is much more expensive than buying stock market investments. With shares the stamp duty is just 0.5% and brokers' commission is usually just a few pounds.

Thanks to the second tax change, borrowing to invest in property has become much less attractive, especially now that interest rates have increased significantly. Higher-rate tax relief for mortgage interest has been taken away and in its place landlords receive a "tax reduction" equal to just 20% of their finance costs.

The tax relief restriction only affects *residential* property businesses and does not apply to properties held inside companies.

The restriction to tax relief on interest costs is even more painful than the stamp duty increase because those affected feel its impact every year, not just when a new property is purchased.

See the Taxcafe guide *How to Save Property Tax* for more information.

Let's take a look at an example where the individual ends up better off by tapping their pension savings to invest in property (although some of the assumptions are questionable):

Example

Hannah is 55, a higher-rate taxpayer and has a pension pot worth £85,000. She decides to withdraw all the money to pay the deposits on two buy-to-let properties which she thinks will perform better than her pension investments over the next 10 years.

The first 25% she withdraws is tax free and the rest is taxed at 40%, leaving her with a grand total of £59,500. Note, she will have to withdraw the money over more than one tax year to avoid going over the £100,000 threshold, which would result in a significant additional tax charge from the loss of her personal allowance.

(Withdrawing taxable income from her pension so many years before she retires is extremely aggressive. It means her future pension contributions will be limited to just £4,000 per year – see Chapter 8.)

Using buy-to-let mortgages she acquires two properties for £100,000 each, with a £25,000 deposit and £75,000 mortgage on each property. The final £9,500 of her pension savings is used to cover her purchase costs (including stamp duty land tax of £6,000 and legal fees).

To make the example simple we'll assume she breaks even on the rental income side. All of Hannah's rental income goes towards paying mortgage interest, income tax and other costs associated with the property. Note, now that interest rates have increased significantly it's extremely likely that she will incur an overall rental loss, which means she will have to find money from other sources to cover her costs.

We'll assume Hannah's properties grow by roughly 7% per year. 10 years' later, when she's 65, they're worth £400,000 in total. She decides to sell one property to pay off both mortgages and use the second property for retirement income. On the £200,000 property she sells she faces a capital gains tax bill and other selling costs of roughly £30,000. After paying off both mortgages (£150,000 in total) she's left with £20,000 in the bank and a fully paid up property worth £200,000.

How would she have fared by keeping her pension investments instead? If we assume they also would have grown by roughly 7% per year, after 10 years she'd end up with around £170,000. She could withdraw 25%

tax free and, assuming the rest was withdrawn gradually and taxed at just 20%, she would end up with £144,500 in total.

In summary, with a pension she ends up with £144,500, with property she ends up with £220,000 – over 50% better off.

Hannah does much better with property despite paying 40% tax on all the money she takes out of her pension to fund the purchases and despite having to pay capital gains tax when she sells one of the properties.

Of course, the only reason the properties did better is because they were heavily geared up with borrowed money and then rose in value. This is an extremely high-risk strategy and probably only suitable for experienced property investors who are many years away from retirement (i.e. closer to 55 than 65).

Geared investments almost always do better than ungeared investments when things go to plan and the assets rise in value. If the properties had fallen in value significantly, Hannah could have lost all of her capital.

While borrowing heavily to invest in property worked when interest rates were low, now that interest rates have increased significantly, coupled with the fact that tax relief on mortgage interest is restricted, it is much harder to make an overall rental profit on a heavily geared property investment.

In many cases property investors with big mortgages like Hannah will be making rental losses, which means they will require money from other sources to subsidize their property investments.

What about using your pension savings to invest in property without a mortgage? Let's take a look at a simple example:

Example
Bill is 65 and retired and has a pension pot worth £150,000 (he has already taken his tax-free lump sum), as well as other taxable income of roughly £25,000 per year.

He currently withdraws the income generated by his pension investments but wants to keep the capital intact for his children. His pension savings are invested in funds earning income of £6,000 per year (£4,800 after paying 20% income tax on the pension withdrawal).

He wants to know if he could get more income by withdrawing all the money from his pension and buying a rental property outright without a mortgage.

If he withdraws all his pension pot in one go he'll pay 40% income tax on most of the money. He will also lose his personal allowance and some of the money will be taxed at 45%. So we'll assume he withdraws £50,000 per year over three tax years, paying basic-rate tax on around half his withdrawals and 40% tax on the rest, leaving him with roughly £105,000.

He then buys a rental property for £100,000, using the final £5,000 to cover his stamp duty and legal fees. If the property is to earn more income than his pension investments (£6,000) it will need to have a rental yield significantly higher than 6%. That's because with property there are lots of additional costs (repairs, insurance, letting agent fees etc) and there are bound to be empty periods as well.

It is possible to find properties with higher rental yields (in some parts of the country they are higher, in others parts they are lower) but it's probably unlikely Bill will end up with *significantly* more income after deducting the various expenses he will incur.

The problem with using pension savings to buy an expensive asset like property outright is that it may be necessary to spread the withdrawals over many tax years to avoid paying income tax at 40% or more.

And what about Bill's children? When he dies they'll either inherit a pension pot worth £150,000 or a property worth £100,000, plus any capital growth on the investments. Whether they're better off with a pension pot or property will depend on Bill's inheritance tax status and the amount of income tax the children pay.

Let's say Bill's pension pot would be worth £225,000 when he dies after reaching age 75 and his property would be worth £150,000 (i.e. they have both grown by 50%).

If Bill's property is not subject to inheritance tax, his children will inherit the £150,000 asset outright, with no capital gains tax payable if they sell it immediately. Alternatively they will inherit his £225,000 pension pot with income tax payable on any withdrawals, leaving them with either £180,000 (if they pay 20% income tax) or £135,000 (if they pay 40% income tax).

If Bill's property is subject to 40% inheritance tax, his children will inherit £90,000. Alternatively they will inherit his pension pot and, as before, be left with either £180,000 (after paying 20% income tax) or £135,000 (after paying 40% income tax).

In this example the children are only better off with the property if there is no inheritance tax payable and they pay income tax at 40%. Of course, they wouldn't have to withdraw the pension savings they inherit immediately. The money could be left to grow tax free for as long as they like, perhaps until they themselves retire.

In summary, it is possible to deplete your pension savings to invest in property. However, this strategy is only likely to leave you better off if you're prepared to accept much more risk (i.e. borrow money) or you expect property to deliver significantly higher returns than pension investments (typically shares and bonds).

Chapter 13

Drawdown versus Annuities

When you retire you may prefer to use your retirement savings to buy an annuity, rather than use flexi-access drawdown (see Chapter 8).

Annuities often get a bad rap in the press but offer an important benefit: a guaranteed income for life. This may appeal to older retirees who don't want the hassle of managing investments and desire what is as close as it gets to a risk-free income.

Annuity rates were very low for many years but have become a lot more attractive following recent increases in interest rates. The life insurance companies that offer annuities take your cash and invest it in long-term gilts (debt issued by the UK Government). As long-term gilt yields increase, so too do annuity rates.

Although annuities have become more attractive in recent times, they're seen by many as a bit of a con. The idea is lots of retirees pool their money together and those that live longer than average are subsidized by those who live shorter than average. That's fair enough but what many people suspect is that annuity providers skim off a big chunk of the money in charges.

There are lots of misconceptions about annuities and it's likely they will form part of many individuals' retirement plans in the years ahead.

And the choice between drawdown and annuities doesn't have to be an all or nothing one. Some retirees may use some of their pension savings to purchase an annuity, so that they have some guaranteed income, and keep their remaining savings in drawdown to top up their income and cover one-off expenses.

At some point in the future rules may be introduced once again that cap the amount of income you can withdraw from your pension, or force you to use your pension savings to obtain some sort of guaranteed income. This could happen if the Government thinks drawdown pension pots are being depleted too quickly.

Whatever the merits of annuities, there are several reasons why flexi-access drawdown may be more attractive than buying an annuity immediately when you retire:

Benefit #1 – Take the Tax-free Cash and Keep Working

When you reach age 55 you may want to get your hands on your 25% tax-free lump sum but keep working for another 10 years or even longer.

Any additional income you take from your pension pot while you are still working (e.g. annuity income) could be taxed at 40% or more if you also have income from a job or business.

Because there is no requirement to withdraw income from a flexi-access drawdown arrangement, you can postpone withdrawing income until you actually retire and your income tax rate falls.

While you are working your pension savings can continue to grow tax free.

Benefit #2 – Keep Your Favourite Investments

If you opt for an annuity you generally have to sell your pension investments and hand over your savings to an insurance company.

This is not an attractive proposition if you are confident your pension investments will perform well.

With a drawdown pension you can enjoy the best of both worlds: an income and tax-free investment growth on the money left inside your pension plan.

Benefit #3 – Wait for Better Annuity Rates

Many pension experts argue that you should ultimately use your pension savings to buy an annuity because the income is more secure than drawdown income (the income never falls no matter how long you live and no matter what happens to interest rates and the value of investments).

The problem is that annuity rates may be unattractive when you retire.

One solution is to start your retirement with a drawdown pension and make a phased exit by using part of your drawdown money to buy an annuity at regular intervals if interest rates rise further and annuities become more attractive.

However, there is no guarantee that annuity rates will remain as high as they are at present or increase further.

Benefit #4 – Reduce Your Income and Save Tax

If you can vary your income from year to year, as you can with drawdown, you can do some constructive tax planning. This is very useful in years when your tax bill may spike because you receive big one-off receipts such as capital gains.

Let's say you sell a buy-to-let property and the capital gain is £50,000. If you reduce your drawdown income in the same tax year, so that your basic-rate band is not fully utilised, you will pay 18% tax instead of 28% tax on some of your capital gain.

The basic-rate band is currently £37,700 so the maximum potential tax saving from paying 18% capital gains tax instead of 28% tax is currently:

$$£37,700 \times 10\% = £3,770$$

This tax saving could be enjoyed every time you sell a rental property and allows individuals with many properties to wind down their portfolios slowly when they retire.

It is also possible to achieve further capital gains tax savings by spreading property sales across several tax years because this lets you make use of more than one annual CGT exemption.

Unfortunately this additional saving will be smaller in the years ahead because the annual CGT exemption is falling from £12,300 to £6,000 from 6th April 2023 and then to £3,000 from 6th April 2024. Thus the additional annual saving from spreading sales across several tax years will fall from £3,444 at present to £840.

Annuities after Death

If you are receiving income from a bog-standard annuity, no money will be payable to your family (e.g. your children) after you die.

The income payments will continue if you have purchased a joint-life annuity (typically for your spouse) or an annuity which pays out for a guaranteed period.

If you die before age 75, payments made to your beneficiary will be tax free. If you die when you are 75 or older, income paid to your beneficiary will be taxed at their marginal rate.

Part 3

Pensions vs ISAs

Chapter 14

Introduction

Which is better: an ISA or a pension?

This is an important question. ISAs and pensions are the two most popular savings vehicles for individuals.

When it comes to saving tax there are no ifs, buts or maybes: pensions are a **much** more powerful tax shelter for most higher-rate taxpayers.

With ISAs there is no up-front tax relief on the money you put in but withdrawals are tax free. With pensions there is up-front tax relief but most withdrawals are taxed.

At first glance the two tax reliefs appear quite different but, as it happens, tax-free withdrawals (ISAs) and up-front tax relief (pensions) produce exactly the same result, even though the tax savings are enjoyed at different points in time.

However, there are two reasons why pensions are a much better tax shelter, especially for higher-rate taxpayers:

- **Tax-free lump sum**. Not all of your pension withdrawals are taxed. You can take one quarter as a tax-free lump sum.

- **Retirees usually pay less tax**. If your tax rate falls from 40% to 20% when you retire – as it will for most higher-rate taxpayers – a pension could save you a lot more tax than an ISA. This is because you will enjoy 40% tax relief on the money you put in but will pay no more than 20% tax on the money you take out.

Thanks to these two factors it is quite possible that a pension will generate 41.67% more after-tax income than an ISA, as we shall see in Chapter 15.

Other Tax Differences

Apart from these major tax differences, pensions and ISAs are treated differently in other respects which may be important in some circumstances.

Interest on Cash Balances

While it has always been possible to hold cash in a stocks and shares ISA, any interest was in effect paid net of basic-rate tax. Interest earned in a pension has always been tax free.

This has changed and interest on cash held in a stocks and shares ISA is now completely tax-free.

Tax When You Emigrate

If you become non-UK resident your income and capital gains sheltered inside an ISA will continue to be tax free. Tax free in the UK, that is. The amounts may be taxed in your new country of residence. For example, the Isle of Man Government specifically states in its tax return booklet that an ISA's tax-free status "does not apply in the Isle of Man and you should declare any income from these products".

The tax-exempt status of pensions, however, is recognized in most countries, although they are arguably less portable assets (you can withdraw all your ISA savings easily if you emigrate).

Withholding Taxes on Dividends

These days it is easy for stock market investors to buy shares in overseas companies, the most popular being US companies.

It's important to note that dividends from overseas companies are often subject to withholding tax.

In the US the dividend withholding tax rate is 30%. However, in terms of the double tax agreement between the US and UK, the amount of withholding tax can be reduced by completing an IRS form W-8BEN. Most online stockbrokers will handle these forms on your behalf so the process is relatively simple.

However, there is an important difference between US shares held in pensions and ISAs. The double tax agreement provides a specific exemption for pensions, which means US dividends paid to a pension scheme will not have any US withholding tax deducted.

The double tax agreement does not recognize ISAs. ISA investors are subject to the same reduced withholding tax rate as everyone else: 15%.

ISAs – Protection from Greedy Politicians

Although pensions are arguably a better tax shelter, one tax benefit unique to ISAs is protection from future income tax increases.

Money withdrawn from ISAs is tax free, whether those withdrawals take place next year or in 30 years' time. In contrast, if a future UK Government decides to increase income tax rates, you will probably end up paying more tax than you expected on your pension income.

Recent announcements in this respect have not been encouraging. In the November 2022 Autumn Statement we were told that the income tax personal allowance and higher-rate threshold will remain frozen at £12,570 and £50,270 respectively until 6th April 2028, a further two years.

This freeze gives the Government seven years to let inflation erode their value, at a time when inflation is soaring.

The freeze has been implemented despite Rishi Sunak promising, when he was Chancellor of the Exchequer, that "this government is not going to raise the rates of income tax, national insurance, or VAT".

Saying you're not going to raise tax rates and then freezing tax thresholds is a bit like a mugger telling you he's not going to shoot you just before he sticks a knife in your belly.

In Scotland income tax is already higher for many taxpayers. Higher-rate tax is payable once your income exceeds just £43,662, compared with £50,270 in the rest of the UK. The Welsh Assembly has had the power to set its own tax rates since 6th April 2019 but has not made any changes yet.

When it comes to paying tax on your future pension withdrawals it doesn't really matter what Rishi Sunak or any of the current crop of politicians do. They'll probably be long gone when you're taking money out of your pension.

During your long and happy retirement there are likely to be many different governments, all with the power to dictate how much tax you pay on your pension withdrawals. And there's no denying that Britain has had its fair share of barmy taxes. In 1974 the top income tax rate on earnings was 83% and the top rate on investment income was 98%.

Do you believe that no politician will increase your income tax further at any time over the next 20 to 30 years? If you do think significant income tax increases are a possibility, it may be a good idea to put some of your retirement savings into an ISA.

ISAs are not, however, completely immune from politicians. There were rumours in the press in recent years about a lifetime cap being placed on ISA savings to limit the number of 'ISA millionaires'. Nothing has been announced to date.

Help-to-Buy ISA

In the 2015 Budget George Osborne introduced the Help to Buy ISA – a form of cash ISA where the Government adds £50 for every £200 saved towards a deposit for a first property. The maximum Government bonus is £3,000 for those who have saved £12,000.

It is no longer possible to open one of these accounts (the last date was 30th November 2019). However, those who have an existing account can continue contributing up to £200 per month until 30th November 2029.

Savers can withdraw funds from their account if they need them for another purpose but the bonus will only be made available to buy a home.

Lifetime ISA

Those aged 18 to 39 can open a Lifetime ISA which can be used to save for a first home or for retirement.

Any money you put in (up to £4,000 per year) receives a 25% Government bonus. So if you put in £4,000, the Government will add £1,000.

It's possible to continue making contributions up to age 50. This means you can invest up to £128,000 between age 18 and 50 with a Government bonus of up to £32,000.

The bonus is paid monthly.

Contributions to a Lifetime ISA fall within the overall £20,000 ISA subscription limit. In other words, if you invest £4,000 in your Lifetime ISA you will be able to invest another £16,000 in a cash ISA or a stocks and shares ISA.

Lifetime ISAs are available from banks, building societies and investment managers and qualifying investments are the same as for cash ISAs and stocks and shares ISAs.

You can open more than one Lifetime ISA during your lifetime (as long you're under 40) but can only pay into one per tax year.

Lifetime ISAs – Early Withdrawals

Unlike a pension, your savings are not locked up inside a Lifetime ISA. However, if you withdraw money before reaching age 60, for any reason other than to buy your first home, there will normally be a 25% early withdrawal charge.

This will claw back all of the Government bonus, plus an additional 6.25% of the amount you invested.

For example, if you invest £1,000, the Government will add £250, giving you total savings of £1,250. If you then decide to withdraw the money, the 25% penalty will be £312.50, leaving you with £937.50. Thus you will lose the Government bonus plus an extra £62.50 (6.25%) out of the amount you originally invested.

This charge effectively also applies to any growth in the value of your savings.

Where an individual is diagnosed with terminal ill health, they can withdraw all their Lifetime ISA savings tax free (including the bonus), regardless of age.

The early withdrawal charge was reduced temporarily from 25% to 20% between 6th March 2020 and 5th April 2021. This was to help individuals experiencing financial difficulty during the pandemic. It meant you could withdraw your savings without having to pay any additional penalty, all you would lose was the Government bonus.

There are calls to have the early withdrawal penalty permanently removed.

Lifetime ISAs – Buying Your First Home

If you are a first-time homebuyer, funds can be withdrawn 12 months after opening the account. The property must cost no more than £450,000, be located in the UK and your only residence.

The money cannot be used to invest in buy-to-let property.

The account holder will inform their ISA manager that a property is to be purchased and the funds will be paid direct to the solicitor.

If you already have a Help to Buy ISA you can only use the Government bonus from one account to buy your first home. If you have a Help to Buy and Lifetime ISA you could for example:

- Use the Help to Buy ISA with the Government bonus to buy your first home and keep your Lifetime ISA to save for retirement

- Use the Lifetime ISA with the Government bonus to buy your first home and withdraw the money in your Help to Buy ISA (without the government bonus) to also fund the purchase

Lifetime ISAs – Saving for Retirement

If you use your Lifetime ISA to save for retirement, funds can be withdrawn from age 60.

As we shall see in Chapter 15, a Lifetime ISA could be an attractive alternative to saving in a pension if you are a basic-rate taxpayer. Like pensions they attract a top up from the Government but, unlike pensions, ALL the money you take out will be tax free.

However, in most cases it would probably be unwise to stop making contributions to a workplace pension scheme because that would also mean giving up your employer's contribution (which is effectively 'free' money).

Lifetime ISAs have the same inheritance tax treatment as other ISAs: when you die the funds will form part of your estate for inheritance tax purposes. However, your spouse will be able to transfer all your ISA savings into their own ISA so that the money continues to grow tax free.

ISAs – Non-tax Benefits

- **Flexibility.** With an ISA you can access your savings *at any time*. You can also withdraw and replace cash from your ISA without it counting towards your annual ISA subscription limit, as long as the repayment is made in the same tax year as the withdrawal. (Note not all ISA providers offer this.) At present pension savers can only access their money when they reach age 55 (rising to age 57 in 2028 and probably higher at some point in the future). Having £100,000 sitting in your pension isn't much use if you need emergency cash.

- **No age limit**. In practice you cannot keep contributing to a pension indefinitely. Once you reach age 75 you will not receive tax relief on your contributions. There is no upper age limit for ISA investments and you can withdraw money and make new contributions continually.

- **No earnings required.** If you want to contribute more than £3,600 per year to a pension with tax relief you need 'earnings'. There is no such restriction on ISA investments, although the maximum annual investment is currently capped at £20,000.

Pensions – Non-tax Benefits

- **Investment limits.** The maximum annual investment is £40,000 and the carry-forward rules allow a contribution of up to £160,000. However, as we saw in Chapter 4, the maximum contribution that you can make with full higher-rate tax relief may be a lot lower than these limits.

- **Investment choice**. Pensions offer a wider choice of investments than ISAs. For example, ISAs cannot be used to invest directly in commercial property whereas pensions can.

- **Protection from creditors**. In the event of bankruptcy, pension savings held inside an HMRC approved pension are generally protected from creditors (most occupational and personal pensions are HMRC approved). Money withdrawn from a pension can potentially be claimed for a period of time.

Chapter 15

Case Study: ISA vs Pension

In this chapter we'll follow two investors building up a retirement nest egg over 10 years and see who ends up better off:

- Peter – Pension investor
- Ian – ISA investor

Both are higher-rate taxpayers and invest £6,000 per year. Peter makes an initial contribution of £8,000 to which the taxman adds a further £2,000 of basic-rate tax relief.

He then claims back £2,000 when completing his tax return. All in all Peter has £10,000 of pension savings that have only cost him £6,000.

Ian also invests £6,000 per year out of his own pocket in an ISA. He doesn't enjoy any tax relief on his contributions so his total investment is just £6,000. Note Ian invests in a traditional ISA. We'll compare pensions and Lifetime ISAs shortly.

Both Peter and Ian enjoy investment returns of 7% per year. These returns are completely tax free for both the ISA investor and the pension investor.

We track how both investors perform from year to year in Table 3. At the end of year 1 they have £10,700 and £6,420 respectively, which is simply their initial investments of £10,000 and £6,000 plus 7% tax-free investment growth.

After five years, Peter has £24,613 more than Ian and after 10 years he has £59,134 more than Ian. Even though they're both earning an identical tax-free return of 7% and investing the same amount of money out of their own pockets, Peter is much better off because his annual investment is boosted by income tax relief on his contributions.

In fact, Ian always has just 60% as much money as Peter. Peter's extra 40% is thanks to the income tax relief he receives on his pension contributions.

Table 3
Pension Savings vs ISA Savings

End Year	Pension £	ISA £
1	10,700	6,420
2	22,149	13,289
3	34,399	20,640
4	47,507	28,504
5	61,533	36,920
6	76,540	45,924
7	92,598	55,559
8	109,780	65,868
9	128,164	76,899
10	147,836	88,702

After-tax Comparison

Although Ian's retirement savings are much smaller than Peter's, that's not the whole story. Firstly, Ian enjoyed much more flexibility along the way and could have taken money out of his ISA at any time. Peter can only withdraw money from his pension when he's 55 or older.

Secondly, Ian can withdraw all his ISA savings *tax free*. Peter will have to pay income tax on any money he withdraws over and above his 25% tax-free lump sum.

If he withdraws all his pension savings in one go he'll pay income tax at 40% on a lot of the money. However, because these are *retirement savings* we will assume Peter only withdraws a little bit of money each year to avoid depleting his capital too quickly and pays income tax at the 20% basic rate.

But before we do this let's pretend Peter has to pay 40% tax on all his pension withdrawals and the pension rules do not allow for tax-free lump sums. How would ISAs and pensions compare then?

40% Tax, No Tax-Free Lump Sum

After paying 40% tax on all of his withdrawals Peter the pension saver would be left with £88,702:

$$£147,836 \text{ less } 40\% \text{ tax} = £88,702$$

Ian the ISA investor is left in an identical position:

$$£88,702 \text{ less } 0\% \text{ tax} = £88,702$$

Thus, if you enjoy 40% tax relief on your contributions but pay 40% tax on your withdrawals, an ISA and pension will provide identical tax savings – if we ignore the tax-free lump sum.

40% Tax, Tax-Free Lump Sum

Of course, in practice Peter can take a 25% tax-free lump sum of £36,959 (£147,836 x 25%). He'll only pay tax on the remaining £110,877.

If we assume he pays 40% tax on the rest of his pension withdrawals his position after tax is as follows:

Tax-free lump sum:	£36,959
After-tax income (£110,877 less 40% tax):	£66,526

Peter is left with a total of £103,485 compared with Ian the ISA investor's £88,702.

This means Peter has 16.67% more money than Ian.

So even if you pay 40% tax on all of your pension income when you retire you will still receive more after-tax income from a pension than an ISA, thanks to the tax-free lump sum.

You could end up paying tax at 40% on some or all of your pension withdrawals if you have a significant amount of income from other sources, for example from rental property.

You could also end up paying tax at 40% on some of your withdrawals if you have built up a large pension pot and therefore have a large pension income.

20% Tax and Tax-Free Lump Sum

Finally, we'll assume that Peter, like most other retirees, is a basic-rate taxpayer when he retires. Peter's after-tax position is now as follows:

Tax-free lump sum:	£36,959
After-tax income (£110,877 less 20% tax):	£88,702

Peter is left with a total of £125,661 compared with Ian the ISA investor's £88,702.

Peter the pension saver ends up with 41.67% more money than Ian the ISA investor.

This example shows that, if you are a higher-rate taxpayer while you are saving for retirement and a basic-rate taxpayer when you retire, you will end up significantly better off using a pension instead of an ISA to save for retirement.

Tax-Free Pension Withdrawals

In the above example Peter pays 20% income tax on all of his pension income. The implicit assumption is that his income tax personal allowance is used up by other taxable income, perhaps his state pension and income from rental properties or a part-time job or part-time business.

I taxed all of his private pension income at 20% because I did not want to overstate the benefits of pension saving. In reality, some of the income you receive from a private pension plan may be tax free thanks to your income tax personal allowance.

The income tax personal allowance for the current tax year is £12,570. It will remain frozen at this level until 5th April 2028.

There used to be additional age-related personal allowances for older taxpayers but these have now been almost completely phased out. Nevertheless, even with just the standard income tax personal allowance, many retirees will receive some of the income they withdraw from their pension tax free.

Once you reach state pension age your state pension could use up a big chunk of your personal allowance. However, you can start withdrawing income from your other pensions roughly 10 years earlier.

If during this period your taxable income from other sources (e.g. rental property) does not use up all of your personal allowance, some of your pension income will be tax free.

If some of your pension income will be tax free, this naturally makes pensions even more attractive than ISAs for retirement saving.

Basic-Rate Taxpayers

In the above examples Ian and Peter were both higher-rate taxpayers when they were making contributions. How do pensions and ISAs compare if you're a basic-rate taxpayer (income under £50,270 at present) and only enjoy basic-rate tax relief?

Let's assume that Ian and Peter are basic-rate taxpayers. Ian has £1,000 to invest in an ISA, Peter has £1,000 to invest in a pension.

Peter makes a cash contribution of £1,000 and the taxman adds £250 of basic-rate relief, leaving him with total pension savings of £1,250. Ian invests £1,000 in an ISA but doesn't receive any tax relief on his contributions so his total savings come to £1,000.

Now as it happens we can completely ignore any further contributions they may decide to make and their investment returns. These do not alter the outcome in any way.

In the previous examples we compared the fortunes of Ian and Peter after they had made contributions for 10 years. However, the final outcome would have been exactly the same after one year, two years or any number of years.

Their investment returns are also irrelevant as long as we assume that they enjoy identical tax-free returns. This is a reasonable assumption to make because pension and ISA savings can be invested largely in the same types of asset (if anything pensions offer a bit more flexibility, for example by allowing you to invest in commercial property).

Basic-Rate Taxpayer in Retirement

If we assume that Peter the pension saver is also a basic-rate taxpayer when he retires his after-tax position will be as follows:

Tax-free lump sum:	£312.50
After-tax income (£937.50 less 20% tax):	£750

Peter is left with a total of £1,062.50 compared with Ian the ISA investor's £1,000.

Peter is just 6.25% better off than Ian.

If you ask me this is not sufficient reward for putting your money in a locked box until you are at least 55. It's one reason why some basic-rate taxpayers may consider postponing contributions until they become higher-rate taxpayers (see Chapter 17).

Investing in a pension will, however, be more appealing if Peter expects some of his taxable pension income to be covered by his personal allowance or, more importantly, if he belongs to a workplace pension scheme and his employer is making additional contributions.

Higher-Rate Taxpayer in Retirement

What if Peter is a basic-rate taxpayer when he is making pension contributions but ends up paying higher-rate tax on all of his pension income?

This could happen if, for example, he eventually inherits or accumulates a significant amount of other assets such as rental property, or if the Government reduces the higher-rate threshold.

His after-tax position will then be as follows:

Tax-free lump sum:	£312.50
After-tax income (£937.50 less 40% tax):	£562.50

Peter is left with a total of £875 compared with Ian the ISA investor's £1,000.

Peter is 12.5% worse off than Ian.

This is the worse possible outcome when it comes to saving in a pension. And I don't think it's a completely unrealistic outcome. There are surely many pension savers out there who are enjoying just basic-rate tax relief on their contributions but will ultimately pay 40% tax when they withdraw those same contributions.

Summary

Pensions are extremely valuable tax shelters *in the right circumstances.* They're most attractive when you enjoy higher-rate tax relief (40%) on your contributions but only pay basic-rate tax (20%) on your taxable withdrawals. In this case you could end up with 41.67% more income that someone who uses an ISA to save for retirement.

The various examples we have looked at are summarised in the table below. For example, someone who enjoys higher-rate tax relief on their contributions and also pays higher-rate tax on all of their taxable withdrawals could end up with 16.67% more income that someone who uses an ISA to save for retirement.

	Basic-rate tax	Higher-rate tax
Basic-rate relief	6.25%	-12.5%
Higher-rate relief	41.67%	16.67%

Remember too that pensions are also more attractive if you expect some of your taxable withdrawals to be covered by your personal allowance or if you also receive contributions from your employer.

Freezing the Higher-Rate Threshold

Throughout this guide I have stated that "at present most retirees are basic-rate taxpayers". While this will remain true for most individuals it's possible that many readers will end up as higher-rate taxpayers when they retire.

This is because the Government has frozen the higher-rate threshold for seven years until 5th April 2028. And this tax policy has been introduced at a time when inflation is running at its highest rate in decades.

For example, if inflation averages around 5% per year throughout the seven year freeze, by 5th April 2028 it will take an income of around £67,000 to purchase what £50,270 would have bought you at the start. The difference is that, with an income of £67,000, you would be a higher-rate taxpayer, paying 40% tax on around £13,000 of your income, even though your income has not risen in real terms.

Thus, in the future, some pension savers, who expected to pay no more than 20% tax on their pension withdrawals, will pay 40% tax on *some* of their withdrawals.

Those wealthier pension savers who already expected to pay 40% tax on some of their pension withdrawals will now pay 40% tax on *more* of their withdrawals.

Some individuals who are currently basic-rate taxpayers, receiving just basic-rate tax relief on their pension contributions, may end up paying higher-rate tax on some of their pension withdrawals.

The freeze in the higher-rate threshold will thus alter the relative attractiveness of pensions over other savings products.

Lifetime ISA vs Pension

Those aged 18 to 39 can open a Lifetime ISA which can be used to save for a first home or for retirement.

It's possible to invest up to £4,000 per year with a 25% Government bonus and continue contributing up to age 50.

The Lifetime ISA is an attractive alternative to saving in a pension if you are a basic-rate taxpayer. Like pensions they attract a top up from the Government but, unlike pensions, ALL the money you take out will be tax free.

For example, if you are a basic-rate taxpayer and invest £1,000 in either a pension or a Lifetime ISA you will receive a £250 top up from the taxman, leaving you with £1,250 in either account.

When you retire, however, withdrawals from the Lifetime ISA will be tax free, whereas only 25% of the money withdrawn from the pension will be tax free. The rest will be subject to income tax (although some of your pension income may also be tax free thanks to your personal allowance).

Let's say you pay tax at the 20% basic rate on your pension income. If we ignore investment growth to keep the example simple (it doesn't affect the outcome), with a Lifetime ISA you will end up with £1,250, with a pension you will end up with just £1,063 after tax.

Thus, if you're a basic-rate taxpayer, your retirement income could be 17.6% higher with a Lifetime ISA.

Lifetime ISA vs Pension – Higher-rate Taxpayers

Higher-rate taxpayers will generally get more bang for their buck from a pension.

For example, if you invest £1,000 in a Lifetime ISA you will receive a £250 top up from the Government leaving you with £1,250.

Because higher-rate taxpayers also receive a tax refund when they contribute to a pension (higher-rate tax relief) they can make bigger initial contributions. For example, if you invest £1,333 in a pension (£1,000/0.75) you'll receive a £333 top up from the Government, leaving you with £1,666 in your pension.

You will also receive higher-rate relief of £333 (£1,666 x 20%) so, as with a Lifetime ISA, the investment will only cost you £1,000 personally (£1,333 personal investment - £333 higher-rate relief).

Ignoring investment growth, when you retire your £1,666 pension pot will become £1,416 (after taking 25% tax free and assuming the rest is taxed at 20%), compared with the £1,250 you would receive from a Lifetime ISA.

Thus, your retirement income could be 13% higher with a pension.

But if you end up paying higher-rate tax on all of your pension income (for example if you have a lot of income from other sources, e.g. rental property) you will end up with only £1,166 from a pension, compared with £1,250 from a Lifetime ISA.

Thus your retirement income could be 7% higher with a Lifetime ISA.

There are other important differences between Lifetime ISAs and pensions. With pensions your money is locked up until you're 55 (rising to 57 in 2028 and possibly higher in future years). With Lifetime ISAs you'll lose the Government top up and normally pay a penalty if you withdraw anything before age 60, unless the money is used to buy your first home. The rest of your savings can be withdrawn at any time.

If the pension is a company scheme, the additional contribution from your employer will make investing in such a scheme more attractive than a Lifetime ISA in most circumstances.

In other words, you should probably not opt out of your employer's pension scheme to invest in a Lifetime ISA.

Make Mine a Double!

It *may* be possible to invest in a Lifetime ISA and then, when you're 60, take the money out and stick it into a pension, thereby enjoying two rounds of tax relief.

For example, if you invest £1,000 in a Lifetime ISA you will receive a 25% Government bonus, leaving you with £1,250. Ignoring investment growth, when you're 60 you will be able to withdraw the £1,250 tax free and may be able to invest it in a pension.

Because higher-rate taxpayers also receive a tax refund when they contribute to a pension (higher-rate tax relief), they can make bigger initial contributions. So instead of investing just your Lifetime ISA savings of £1,250 in your pension, you may be able to invest £1,667 (£1,250/0.75).

You'll receive £417 of basic-rate tax relief from the taxman, leaving you with £2,084 in your pension. You will also receive higher-rate relief of £417 (£2,084 x 20%), so the investment will only cost you £1,250 personally (the amount withdrawn from the Lifetime ISA).

Ignoring investment growth, when you eventually retire your £2,084 pension pot will become £1,771 (after taking 25% tax free and the rest taxed at 20%), compared with the £1,250 you would receive from your Lifetime ISA alone.

Thus, your retirement income could be 42% higher than someone who invests in a Lifetime ISA only.

And your retirement income will be 77% higher than someone who invests in a traditional ISA only (ignoring investment growth they would end up with just £1,000).

It's impossible to say whether anyone will be able to benefit from this potential "tax loophole".

Because only those who are under 40 can open a Lifetime ISA and because withdrawals will only be possible from age 60, it will be many years before anyone can perform this tax relief double! Tax and pension rules will no doubt change a lot between now and then.

Chapter 16

ISAs vs Pensions: Death Tax Planning

Your Spouse

There is no inheritance tax on assets, including ISAs, left to your spouse.

Your spouse can inherit your ISA savings and invest them in their own ISA, so any future income and capital gains will continue to be tax free.

This was not possible a few years ago – your spouse could inherit your ISA savings but they were taken out of the ISA wrapper.

What happens now is your spouse will receive a special expanded ISA allowance when you die which will allow them to put all your ISA savings into their own ISA.

This tax concession is available to married couples and civil partners but is not available to unmarried couples.

How do ISAs compare with pensions?

Your spouse or unmarried partner can inherit your pension pot and withdraw money from it as and when they like. The investments inside the pension will continue to grow tax free.

If you die before age 75 your spouse or partner can withdraw all the money tax free. If you die after reaching age 75 they will pay income tax on any money they take out.

If your spouse or partner already has significant pension savings or other taxable income of their own and inherits a second pension pot from you, it is possible that any additional withdrawals they make from the second pension pot will take them over the higher-rate threshold and be taxed at 40%.

For this reason it may be preferable, in some cases, for married couples to run down their pension savings rather than their ISA savings, as long as no more than 20% basic rate tax is paid on the pension withdrawals.

The surviving spouse can then inherit a larger quantity of ISA savings and make tax-free withdrawals from them.

Unmarried couples who inherit ISA savings cannot keep them inside the tax wrapper. This means they may pay tax on any *future* income and capital gains. However, the surviving partner can gradually reinvest the inherited money in their own ISA.

Passing on ISA savings may not be the most tax efficient route when it comes to leaving money to your children.

Your Children

When you die your ISAs will form part of your estate for inheritance tax purposes (although certain AIM shares are exempt after two years).

Inheritance tax at 40% is payable on assets that exceed the threshold – currently £325,000 but up to £650,000 for married couples. An additional nil rate band of £175,000 is also available for the family home (up to £350,000 for married couples).

If your ISA savings are not subject to inheritance tax your children will effectively inherit a tax-free lump sum, although the money will be inherited outside the ISA tax wrapper.

If your children inherit your pension pot there is usually no inheritance tax payable. They can then withdraw money from it as and when they like. The investments inside the pension will continue to grow tax free.

If you die before age 75 your children can withdraw all the pension money tax free. If you die after reaching age 75 they will pay income tax on any money they take out.

If your children are working when they inherit your pension savings, there's a good chance they will end up paying 40% income tax on any money they take out, unless they leave the money untouched until they themselves retire (and hopefully pay basic-rate tax only).

In summary, if your estate will not be subject to inheritance tax your children may be better off inheriting your ISAs rather than your pension.

If your estate is subject to inheritance tax they may be better off, pound for pound, inheriting your pension savings – but only if they will pay less than 40% tax when they take the money out.

Are ISAs Still a Good Investment?

In Chapter 15 it was shown that pensions are usually a much better tax shelter than ISAs (although a Lifetime ISA will be better for some taxpayers). However, there are 17 million ISA savers in Britain and I'm one of them!

What attracts so many people to ISAs is their flexibility. You can withdraw money at any time. Pension investors have to wait until they reach the minimum retirement age of 55 or older.

As with everything in life, a compromise is usually the best solution. There's no harm in using both.

And as we will see in the next two chapters, an ISA may be a great place to park money **before** you invest it in a pension.

Postponing & Accelerating Pension Saving

Chapter 17

Basic-Rate Taxpayers: Should They Make Pension Contributions?

Financial advisors usually advise people to start making pension contributions as early as possible. They often point to the 'magic' of compound interest. Compound interest – earning interest on interest – seems to possess magical powers, making millionaires out of just about anyone who starts early enough.

However, it's important to not confuse saving in a pension with saving *generally*. It's never too early to start saving... but it may be too early to start saving in a pension.

In previous chapters I have shown that higher-rate taxpayers enjoy twice as much tax relief on their pension contributions as basic-rate taxpayers. A higher-rate taxpayer is currently someone who has taxable income of more than £50,270 (£43,662 in Scotland).

So the question is: should you delay making pension contributions if you are currently a basic-rate taxpayer but expect to become a higher-rate taxpayer in the future?

More specifically, should you invest your savings somewhere else, for example in an ISA, and transfer the money into a pension when you will enjoy much more income tax relief?

This is the question we will answer in this chapter.

Are You a Temporary Basic-Rate Taxpayer?

There are lots of reasons why an individual may be a basic-rate taxpayer in one tax year but a higher-rate taxpayer in another. The most obvious reason is career progression: a graduate earns a lot less income than someone with the same qualifications and 20 years' experience. You may start your working life as a basic-rate taxpayer and become a higher-rate taxpayer a few years later.

Many self-employed business owners who are normally higher-rate taxpayers may become basic-rate taxpayers from time to time, for example if their income falls during an economic downturn or if they have higher than normal tax-deductible expenditure, for example if they make significant investments in equipment during the tax year. Many company directors are also basic-rate taxpayers in some years but higher-rate taxpayers in other years, for example if they pay themselves a small dividend during one tax year and a big dividend during another tax year.

Finally, with the Government freezing the higher-rate threshold at £50,270 for seven years (from 6th April 2021 to 5th April 2028), many people who are currently basic-rate taxpayers will become higher-rate taxpayers in the years ahead, even if their pay simply increases with inflation. (Similarly, many existing higher-rate taxpayers will have more of their income taxed at 40%, allowing them to make bigger pension contributions with 40% tax relief.)

Wealth Warning

There is one group of individuals who should always consider making pension contributions, even if they are only temporary basic-rate taxpayers: company employees who belong to workplace pension schemes. For them tax relief is only one of the benefits of making pension contributions. The employer will often match, or more than match, the contribution made by the employee – effectively handing over free cash which no sensible person would turn down (more on this in Chapter 22).

Case Study – Postponing Pension Contributions

Penny and Isabella are both basic-rate taxpayers but expect to be higher-rate taxpayers in three years' time. Both want to save £3,000 per year but they have different strategies. Penny decides to put her savings in a personal pension straight away because her father has advised her to start saving for retirement as soon as possible. Isabella also wants to save for her retirement but she also wants to maximise her tax relief. She decides to invest in an ISA until she is a higher-rate taxpayer and then transfer the money into a pension.

Who ends up better off?

Table 4
Pension vs ISA
Temporary Basic-Rate Taxpayers

End Year	Pension £	ISA £
1	4,013	3,210
2	8,306	6,645
3	12,900	10,320

We'll assume they both enjoy investment returns of 7% per year (tax-free inside both an ISA and pension). Penny's £3,000 annual investment is topped up with £750 of free cash from the taxman so her gross pension contribution is £3,750. After a year this will have grown to £4,013. After three years she will have £12,900.

Isabella's £3,000 ISA investment will be worth £3,210 after one year. After three years she will have £10,320. The results are summarised in Table 4. For every £1 Penny has in her pension, Isabella has just 80p – the difference is down to the 20% basic-rate tax relief Penny enjoys on her pension contributions.

Becoming Higher-rate Taxpayers

It's the start of the fourth tax year and Isabella knows she will be a higher-rate taxpayer this year. So she decides to take her £10,320 ISA savings and stick them into her pension plan. The taxman will add £2,580 in basic-rate tax relief and, hey presto, she has £12,900 sitting in her pension plan, just like Penny.

However, as a higher-rate taxpayer, Isabella will also receive higher-rate tax relief when she submits her tax return. To calculate this we simply multiply her gross pension contribution by 20%:

£12,900 x 20% = £2,580

In summary, Penny and Isabella have both saved exactly the same amount of money but because Isabella waited until she became a higher-rate taxpayer before making pension contributions she ends up with £2,580 more than Penny.

Maximising the Pension Pot

In the above example Isabella has the same amount of money as Penny in her pension plus a tax refund from HMRC. However, if Isabella would prefer to maximise her pension savings she could do things slightly differently.

What she could do is make a bigger pension contribution – £13,760 instead of just her £10,320 ISA savings. The taxman will top this up with £3,440 to produce a gross pension contribution of £17,200.

Isabella won't be out of pocket despite making a bigger contribution because she will also receive a tax refund of £3,440 (£17,200 x 20%) – her higher-rate relief.

This means the amount she personally contributes will simply be the amount she has saved up in her ISA:

£13,760 pension contribution *minus* £3,440 tax refund = £10,320

Now look at the size of Isabella's pension pot. She has £17,200 compared with Penny's £12,900 – 33% more money!

33% – The Magic Number

The same 33% increase in pension savings can be enjoyed by anyone who postpones making pension contributions while temporarily a basic-rate taxpayer.

Regardless of whether you postpone for one year, 10 years or any other time period, and regardless of whether you are making big or small pension contributions, the result is exactly the same:

Your pension pot will be 33% bigger

Finally, remember that, although Isabella postpones her pension contributions, she does NOT postpone saving. Note too that she invests in an ISA so that, like Penny, she does not miss out on tax-free growth.

Practical Pointers

- The assumption is that Isabella enjoys the maximum higher-rate tax relief on her £17,200 pension contribution. However, we know from Chapter 4 that Isabella will only enjoy full higher-rate tax relief if she also has at least £17,200 of income taxed at 40%. If she doesn't, she will have to spread her pension contributions over more than one tax year.

- Isabella personally contributes £13,760, which is more than her £10,320 ISA savings. However, when she gets her tax refund back she is not left out of pocket. How do we calculate the number £13,760? Simply divide £10,320 by 0.75.

Chapter 18

Higher-Rate Taxpayers: Can They Put Off Pension Saving?

In the previous chapter I showed how basic-rate taxpayers may be better off postponing pension contributions until they become higher-rate taxpayers. What about higher-rate taxpayers – can they also put off making pension contributions?

Be careful about asking a financial advisor this question by the way. It's like giving Superman Kryptonite. They usually advise people to start making pension contributions as soon as possible. However, as I pointed out in the previous chapter, it's important to not confuse the benefits of saving in a pension with the benefits of saving *generally*.

There are lots of reasons why you might not feel like putting money into a pension right now, even though you would receive lots of tax relief. It all revolves around the potentially lengthy jail sentence placed on pension savings – you can't access them until you are 55 or older.

If you have big financial commitments, for example a mortgage or children's education to pay for many years, you may be very reluctant to tie up your savings in a pension.

You certainly shouldn't be making any pension contributions if you are in imminent danger of losing a big chunk or all of your income, for example if your business is struggling or you are worried about losing your job.

Am I saying it's not necessary to save in these situations? No, I'm a big fan of saving from day one. What I am saying is that you don't necessarily have to save via a pension... not at certain stages of your life at least. It's a fat lot of good having £100,000 in your pension pot if your home is about to be repossessed.

Before making any pension contributions, you should always make sure you have a significant amount of money saved elsewhere to protect against:

- An unforeseen drop in income, and
- Unforeseen expenses

But what about all the tax savings enjoyed by pension savers? If you delay putting money into a pension, won't you lose out? This is one of the great misconceptions about pensions.

As it happens, if you want immediate access to your savings, you don't have to put money into a pension until you are ready.

You will not be one penny worse off than someone who makes pension contributions continually for many years.

I've never heard any pension experts make this crucial point. Maybe it's because advising people to put off making pension contributions is bad for business, a bit like a tobacco company telling you to quit smoking.

Case Study – Postponing Pension Contributions

In Chapter 15 we compared Peter the pension saver with Ian the ISA investor. What we discovered is that pensions are much more powerful than traditional ISAs – you could end up with at least 41.67% more income from a pension.

However, it is possible that Ian, the ISA investor, will have the last laugh. Let's say he originally started saving into an ISA because he wanted access to his savings. Back then he was worried about losing his job and also had a big mortgage and three children to support. Move forward five years, his career's going well, the mortgage is smaller and the children have all flown the nest.

So he decides to take his ISA savings and stick them into a pension. Is he still worse off than Peter, who started saving in a pension five years earlier?

Table 5
Postponing Pension Contributions
Higher-Rate Taxpayers

End Year	Pension £	ISA £
1	10,700	6,420
2	22,149	13,289
3	34,399	20,640
4	47,507	28,504
5	61,533	36,920

Peter and Ian's savings up to the end of year five are summarised in Table 5. Just to recap, both are higher-rate taxpayers and both personally invest £6,000 per year. Peter enjoys income tax relief so his gross pension contribution is £10,000 per year, compared with Ian's £6,000 ISA investment. They both enjoy tax-free growth of 7% per year. After one year their £10,000 and £6,000 initial investments will be worth £10,700 and £6,420 respectively (explaining the first numbers you see in the table).

After five years Peter has £61,533, compared with Ian's £36,920. Ian now takes his ISA savings and sticks them in a pension. Because he knows he'll get a tax refund (his higher-rate tax relief) he actually makes an investment of £49,226 (£36,920/0.75). The taxman adds £12,307 of basic-rate tax relief and, hey presto, Ian ends up with £61,533 sitting in his pension pot – exactly the same as Peter!

Ian also gets a tax refund of £12,307 (£61,533 x 20%), so his £49,226 pension investment costs him just £36,920 personally – exactly the amount he accumulated in ISAs.

In summary, Peter started saving in a pension from day one, whereas Ian put his savings into an ISA, before transferring the money into a pension five years later. By postponing his pension contributions, Ian was able to access his savings in the event of a financial emergency. Postponing his contributions has not left him out of pocket.

Postponing Pension Contributions – The Dangers

I'm not encouraging anyone to postpone making pension contributions. The point of this exercise is to show that, all things being equal, there is *mathematically* no difference between regular pension contributions and a big catch-up pension contribution. Saving in a pension over many years will not leave you better off.

As with everything, compromise is often the best solution. There's nothing to stop you making some pension contributions now and further catch-up contributions when your personal financial situation is healthier.

There are also some dangers and some very important practical issues when it comes to postponing pension contributions:

Danger # 1 Higher Rate Tax Relief Could Be Scrapped

We discussed this danger in Chapter 6. For many years there have been fears that higher-rate tax relief on pension contributions will be scrapped because it costs the Government so much.

One option would be to give everyone the same flat rate of tax relief, such as 30%. Such a change would be more generous to basic-rate taxpayers but punish higher-rate taxpayers.

Alternatively, higher-rate tax relief could be kept but with the annual allowance reduced from £40,000 to, say, £30,000 or less.

Even if the current Conservative Government makes no changes to pension tax relief, there's nothing to stop a future government making the system less generous. Remember pensions are ultra long-term savings vehicles and your contributions will be made under multiple governments, possibly with widely differing views on tax.

Many higher-rate taxpayers may therefore feel that it is wise to not postpone making pension contributions and make hay while the sun is still shining, i.e. make pension contributions NOW while higher-rate tax relief is still available.

Danger # 2 Loss of Employer Pension Contributions

If you belong to a workplace pension scheme to which your employer is contributing, postponing your own contributions could prove costly: you will lose the free cash being offered by your employer (see Chapter 22).

Danger # 3 Your Earnings Fall

If your income falls and you are no longer a higher-rate taxpayer when the time comes to make catch-up contributions, you will not enjoy any higher-rate tax relief.

This could happen if you own a business that enters a long tough patch or period of decline. It could also happen to a company employee who suffers redundancy and is unable to find another job that pays as well.

Danger # 4 Pension Recycling Rules

If you make larger than normal pension contributions a couple of years before you withdraw tax-free cash from your pension, there is a danger that HMRC will argue that you are recycling your tax-free lump sum.

If the recycling rules are triggered, your tax-free lump sum will be treated as an unauthorised payment, resulting in a tax charge of up to 70% (see Chapter 9).

According to HMRC, the recycling rules will also apply if, instead of funding the pension contribution directly from your tax-free lump sum, you use your available savings to pay the contribution and then use your tax-free lump sum to replenish those savings.

The recycling rules will be triggered if you always intended your tax-free lump sum to be an integral way of paying the increased pension contributions, albeit indirectly.

It's difficult to quantify the risk of triggering the recycling rules but the uncertainty alone is good enough reason to be careful of making bigger than normal pension contributions within a couple of years of withdrawing tax-free cash from your pension.

Practical Issue # 1 Maximising Higher Rate Tax Relief

Ian has to make a gross pension contribution of £61,533 to catch up with Peter. We know from Chapter 4 that to obtain the maximum higher-rate tax relief he must also have at least £61,533 of income taxed at 40%. Most people don't.

The bigger your catch-up contribution, the less likely you are to obtain the maximum higher-rate tax relief. Fortunately, there is a possible solution: Ian could spread his catch-up contributions over several tax years to maximise his higher-rate tax relief. This means he shouldn't leave it too close to retirement to make his catch-up contributions, especially if he also wants to make pension contributions out of his income, in addition to investing his ISA savings.

Practical Issue # 2 Exceeding the Annual Allowance

The bigger your catch-up contribution, the more likely you are to exceed the annual allowance (see Chapter 2). The annual allowance is currently £40,000 but could be reduced in the years ahead.

Fortunately, it is possible to carry forward any unused annual allowance from the three previous tax years, so a gross pension contribution of up to £160,000 is possible, provided you have sufficient relevant UK earnings and belonged to a pension scheme in each of those previous years.

Again, the best practical solution for Ian would probably be to spread his contributions over several tax years.

Practical Issue # 3 Tax Free Growth

Ian is able to catch up with Peter because he also enjoys tax-free investment growth in his ISA. If Ian's savings are taxed, he will end up permanently worse off, even after he puts his savings in a pension.

In summary, it is possible to put off pension saving if you don't want to tie up your money right now... but there are dangers and practical obstacles.

Chapter 19

How to Protect Your Child Benefit

Child benefit is an extremely valuable tax-free gift from the Government to parents. Those who qualify currently receive the following annual payments:

- £1,133.60 for the first child
- £751.40 for each subsequent child

Depending on the number of children, a family can expect to receive the following total child benefit payment:

Children	Total Child Benefit
1	£1,134
2	£1,885
3	£2,636
4	£3,388

plus £751 for each additional child

You can keep receiving child benefit until your children are 16 years of age or until age 20 if they are enrolled in 'relevant education' (the likes of GCSEs, A Levels, and NVQs to level 3, but not degree courses).

That's the good news. The bad news is the Government withdraws the benefit where any member of the household has annual income in excess of £50,000.

The withdrawal operates by levying an income tax charge on the *highest earner* in the household.

How the Child Benefit Charge Works

For every £100 the highest earner's income exceeds £50,000, there is a tax charge equivalent to 1% of the child benefit. So if the highest earner in the household has an income of £51,000, the tax charge is 10% of the child benefit.

For a household with two children this means a tax charge of £188 (£1,885 x 10%).

If the highest earner has an income of £55,000, the tax charge is 50% of the child benefit. For a household with two children this means a tax charge of £942.

Once the highest earner's income reaches £60,000, all the child benefit will effectively have been withdrawn.

As an alternative to the income tax charge, the claimant can choose not to receive child benefit.

1970s Style Tax Rates

Higher-rate tax kicks in at £50,270, so those with income between £50,270 and £60,000 have truly eye-watering marginal tax rates.

For example, let's say the highest earner's taxable income goes up from £55,000 to £56,000.

They will pay £400 more income tax and a 10% child benefit charge – £113 for a household with one child. So the total tax charge on the additional £1,000 is £513 – that's a marginal tax rate of 51%!

And if you think that's bad, take a look at the marginal tax rates suffered by parents with more than one child:

2 Children   59%
3 Children   66%
4 Children   74%

You can typically add an extra 2% to all of the above tax rates to take account of national insurance, if your income is from employment or self-employment. The marginal tax rates for dividends are different.

Not all Income is Equal

The child benefit charge only applies if your 'adjusted net income' is over £50,000.

Adjusted net income includes all income subject to income tax, including employment income, profits from self employment, pensions and income from property, savings and dividends.

Income from tax-free investments like ISAs is excluded. What this means is that a parent with work-related income of £50,000 and tax-free dividends of £10,000 from an ISA will avoid the child benefit charge completely; someone with the same £50,000 of earned income but £10,000 of rental income will effectively lose all of their child benefit.

This makes investments like shares and bonds (that can be sheltered inside an ISA) potentially far more tax efficient than rental property.

For example, that £10,000 in rental income will produce an income tax bill of £4,000 and a child benefit charge of £1,885 for a family with two children. Total rental income net of all taxes is just £4,115.

The ISA investor ends up with 143% more income!

How Pension Contributions Can Help

One of the simplest ways for almost all taxpayers to avoid the child benefit charge is by making pension contributions. This is because your adjusted net income is reduced by your gross pension contributions.

In Chapter 18 we looked at the pros and cons of postponing pension contributions if you are a higher-rate taxpayer. Those in the £50,270-£60,000 income bracket, who are the highest earners in households in receipt of child benefit, should be very wary of postponing pension contributions.

By making pension contributions they can enjoy above average levels of tax relief. Let's take a look at some of the potential tax savings:

Example

Alan has taxable income of £60,000 this year. His wife earns £30,000 and claims child benefit for three children: £2,636. On the top £5,000 slice of his income, Alan faces a £2,000 income tax bill and a child benefit charge of £1,318 (50% of the family's child benefit). Alan's £5,000 is reduced to just £1,682.

Let's focus in on that top £5,000 slice of his income and see how he can reduce the child benefit charge:

Alan personally contributes £4,000 into his pension. The taxman adds £1,000 of basic-rate tax relief, producing a gross pension contribution of £5,000. When Alan submits his tax return he also receives £1,000 of higher-rate tax relief (£5,000 x 20%).

Furthermore, because the pension contribution reduces Alan's adjusted net income to £55,000, the child benefit charge is reduced by £1,318.

Alan therefore enjoys a total of £3,318 tax relief on his £5,000 pension contribution, i.e. 66% tax relief.

He ends up with £5,000 in his pension pot instead of £1,682 in after-tax income.

What this example shows is that many parents in the £50,270-£60,000 bracket will enjoy tax relief on their pension contributions of 51% (one child), 59% (two children) or 66% (three children), compared with the 40% tax relief enjoyed by most other higher-rate taxpayers.

Bigger than Normal Pension Contributions

Those in the £50,270-£60,000 income bracket should consider making bigger than normal pension contributions, in particular if they expect their income to rise above £60,000 in the future or if their children are approaching the age where child benefit will be withdrawn.

Example

Gordon has taxable income of £60,000 this year. His wife earns £30,000 and claims child benefit for two children: £1,885. On the top £10,000 slice of his income, Gordon faces a 59% tax charge: £4,000 income tax and a child benefit charge of £1,885.

Gordon wouldn't normally make a gross pension contribution of more than £5,000 but decides to double his contribution for the current tax year so that he can take advantage of the 59% tax relief available.

He could then suspend making any pension contributions next year, for example if his income rises from £60,000 to £65,000. A £5,000 pension contribution next year would attract just 40% tax relief, compared with the 59% available this year.

Much Bigger than Normal Pension Contributions

Even those with income *over* £60,000 can enjoy above average tax relief by making bigger than normal pension contributions.

Example
Colin has taxable income of £65,000 this year. His wife earns £30,000 and receives child benefit for three children: £2,636. On the top £15,000 slice of his income, Colin faces an £8,582 tax charge: £5,946 income tax and a £2,636 child benefit charge.

If Colin makes a gross pension contribution of £5,000 he will enjoy 40% tax relief, just like most other higher-rate taxpayers. He will not avoid any of the child benefit charge because his adjusted net income will not fall below £60,000.

Fortunately his aunt Doris left him some money so Colin decides to make a much bigger than normal £15,000 gross pension contribution this year and then stop making contributions for a year or two.

Colin's pension contribution attracts £5,946 income tax relief and, by reducing his adjusted net income to £50,000, allows him to entirely avoid the £2,636 child benefit charge. The total tax relief is £8,582 or 57% of his gross pension contribution.

Obviously the higher your income the bigger the pension contribution you have to make to get your income below £60,000 and ultimately down to £50,000. However, for some individuals, including those with income well over £60,000, the tax relief may make it worthwhile.

(Note, because the higher-rate tax threshold is £50,270, Colin only receives higher-rate tax relief on £14,730 of his £15,000 pension contribution: £65,000 - £50,270 = £14,730 x 20% = £2,946.)

130

The key tax planning point is that you shouldn't necessarily think in terms of avoiding the child benefit charge completely or permanently.

For those with income close to £60,000 (or over £60,000 in some cases) it may be more practical to think in terms of reducing only part of the charge or reducing it in some tax years but not others.

Postponing Pension Contributions

In Chapter 17 I argued that some basic-rate taxpayers should consider postponing pension contributions until their income rises above £50,270 and they become higher-rate taxpayers.

With the child benefit charge kicking in close to this income level, this is another reason to consider postponing contributions until your income rises above £50,270. You could then make bigger than normal catch-up contributions which enjoy more tax relief.

In Scotland the higher-rate threshold currently kicks in when your income goes above £43,662, so some higher-rate taxpayers in Scotland may wish to consider postponing pension contributions until their income rises above £50,000.

Couples Pension Planning

Where one spouse or partner is in the £50,000-£60,000 income bracket and the other has a smaller income, it may be worth getting the higher earner to make most of the family's pension contributions, even for just one or two tax years.

Example
Chris and Maria earn £60,000 and £50,000 respectively. They receive child benefit for two children: £1,885. In recent years they've been making pension contributions of £5,000 each. This year the couple decide that Maria should stop her pension contributions and Chris should increase his by £5,000 to £10,000. By making an additional £5,000 pension contribution Chris will avoid an additional 50% child benefit charge, saving the couple £942. Furthermore, with the higher-rate threshold currently £50,270, Maria would not enjoy any higher-rate tax relief on any pension contributions she makes. Chris will enjoy higher-rate tax relief on most of his contribution (except the final £270).

Both Individuals Earn £50,000-£60,000

Where both income earners in the household are in the £50,000-£60,000 bracket, the most tax-efficient strategy is to *equalise* their adjusted net incomes.

Example
Alistair earns £58,000, his wife Wilma earns £55,000. The couple want to make a £5,000 gross pension contribution this year. If Alistair makes the entire contribution this will take his adjusted net income to £53,000. Wilma will then become the household's highest earner with £55,000, resulting in a 50% child benefit charge.

As far as avoiding the child benefit charge is concerned, the best solution may be for Alistair to make a £4,000 gross pension contribution, with Wilma making a £1,000 gross contribution. They will both then have adjusted net income of £54,000 and an additional 10% of their child benefit will be retained.

Of course, many couples will prefer to keep things equal and make identical pension contributions, even if this does not produce the "optimal" tax saving.

The Self-Employed

The taxable income of self-employed individuals (sole traders and business partners) tends to fluctuate more than that of salaried employees and even company owners.

A self-employed individual's taxable income is essentially the pre-tax profits of the business. These will vary from year to year if business conditions improve or decline or if the business owner alters the level of tax deductible spending (e.g. by making investments in tax deductible equipment or vehicles).

As a result some self-employed business owners, who are also parents of qualifying children, may find themselves in the £50,000-£60,000 income bracket in some tax years but not others.

Where possible they should consider always making pension contributions in those '£50,000-£60,000' tax years, possibly contributions that are bigger than normal.

Other Considerations & Drawbacks

To maximise the tax relief on pension contributions it may be necessary to postpone or bring forward contributions or have one household member make bigger contributions than another.

Actions like these may have other consequences that need to be considered. For example, the second member of the household may not be happy about the highest earner accumulating all the retirement savings!

Postponing pension contributions may not be a good idea if this means you forfeit contributions from your employer (see Chapter 22) or if higher-rate tax relief is eventually scrapped (see Chapter 6).

Chapter 20

Higher Income Earners

Income between £100,000 and £125,140

Once your income exceeds £100,000 your income tax personal allowance is gradually taken away. It is reduced by £1 for every £2 you earn above £100,000.

For example, if your income is £110,000 your personal allowance will be reduced by £5,000.

The income tax personal allowance is £12,570 and will remain at this level until 5th April 2028. This means that once your income reaches £125,140 you will have no personal allowance at all.

This is a real tax sting for those earning over £100,000. The personal allowance saves you £5,028 in tax if you are a higher-rate taxpayer.

Paying Tax at 60%

The effect of having your personal allowance taken away is that anyone earning between £100,000 and £125,140 faces a hefty marginal income tax rate of 60%.

For example, someone who earns £100,000 and receives an extra £10,000 will pay 40% tax on the extra income – £4,000.

They'll also have their personal allowance reduced by £5,000, which means they'll have to pay an extra £2,000 in tax (£5,000 x 40%). Total tax on extra income: £6,000 which is 60%.

Saving Tax at 60%

The flipside of this is that anyone in this income bracket who makes pension contributions can enjoy 60% tax relief.

Your personal allowance is reduced if your 'adjusted net income' is more than £100,000. When calculating your adjusted net income you usually deduct any pension contributions you have made.

For example, let's say you have taxable income of £110,000 and invest £8,000 in a pension. For starters you will receive a £2,000 top up from the taxman (your basic-rate tax relief), resulting in a gross pension contribution of £10,000. You'll also receive higher-rate tax relief of £2,000 (£10,000 x 20%).

In addition, by making a gross pension of £10,000 your 'adjusted net income' will be reduced from £110,000 to £100,000, so none of your personal allowance will be taken away. Additional tax saving: £2,000 (£5,000 x 40%).

In summary, your £10,000 pension contribution produces £6,000 of tax savings – a total of 60% tax relief!

Income over £125,140 in 2022/23

This year, when your income rises above £125,140 your marginal income tax rate falls back to 40%. However, making quite big pension contributions can still be attractive because you may still enjoy 60% tax relief on some of the money you put away.

For example, let's say you have taxable income of £135,000 this year and put £28,000 into a pension. Like anyone else you will receive £7,000 basic-rate tax relief, resulting in a gross pension contribution of £35,000. And like any higher-rate taxpayer you will receive £7,000 of higher-rate relief (£35,000 x 20%).

In addition, your £35,000 gross pension contribution will reduce your adjusted net income from £135,000 to £100,000, so none of your personal allowance will be taken away. Additional tax saving: £5,028 (£12,570 x 40%).

In summary, your £35,000 gross pension contribution produces £19,028 of tax savings – a total of 54% tax relief.

Anyone with taxable income of between £125,140 and roughly £150,000 will enjoy more than 50% tax relief this year by making a gross pension contribution that is big enough to take their adjusted net income back down to £100,000.

For example, someone with taxable income of £150,000 who makes a gross pension contribution of £50,000, which takes their adjusted net income back down to £100,000, will enjoy 50.06%

tax relief. Someone with taxable income of £140,000 who makes a gross pension contribution of £40,000 will enjoy 52.6% tax relief.

Although the tax relief is attractive, these are big pension contributions, so in practice this strategy may appeal most to those whose income is only slightly higher than the £125,140 threshold.

Furthermore, if these are one-off big contributions it may be possible to enjoy even more tax relief by postponing them until next year (see below).

Finally, pension contributions in excess of £40,000 will exceed the annual allowance and are only possible if you have unused annual allowance from the three previous tax years.

Additional-Rate Taxpayers

When your income rises above £150,000 this year you become an additional-rate taxpayer and start paying 45% tax on most types of income. The flipside is you can enjoy 45% tax relief on some of your pension contributions (subject to the restriction discussed below).

Starting next year (2023/24) you will become an additional-rate taxpayer when your income rises above £125,140. This tax change was announced in the November 2022 Autumn Statement.

Those on higher incomes will thus generally enjoy tax relief as follows on their pension contributions in future years:

- £50,270-£100,000   40% tax relief
- £100,000-£125,140   60% tax relief
- £125,140 or more   45% tax relief

Those with taxable income between £125,140 and £150,000 currently enjoy 40% tax relief on their pension contributions, rising to 45% next year and in future years. Individuals in this income bracket may therefore wish to consider postponing some of their pension contributions until next year, especially if they can make a big enough contribution next year to recoup some or all of their income tax personal allowance as well. However, there are lots of factors to consider when making such a decision.

The Tapered Annual Allowance

Some high earners taxpayers face restrictions to their pension contributions. The annual allowance can be reduced from £40,000 to just £4,000. Fortunately, the so-called pension taper now kicks in at much higher income levels than previously. As a result, many high earners can enjoy higher pension contributions than before.

Threshold Income

The first thing you have to calculate is your 'threshold income'. If your threshold income is £200,000 or less you are exempt from tapering and can make pension contributions just like anyone else.

Your threshold income is, broadly speaking, your total taxable income. This includes your salary, self-employment profits, dividends, rental profits, interest income and any other taxable income you receive.

From this you deduct any pension contributions you have made *personally* (you deduct the gross contributions).

You can also deduct other reliefs listed in Section 24 of the Income Tax Act 2007. These include things like trade loss relief.

Employer pension contributions are ignored when calculating threshold income. But you must add back any salary sacrificed in exchange for employer pension contributions since 9th July 2015.

The threshold used to be £110,000 but was increased to £200,000 with effect from 6th April 2020.

Example 1
Dirk is self-employed and has taxable income of £225,000 this year (coming mostly from his business and some rental properties). He makes a gross pension contribution of £40,000 into his SIPP (he invests £32,000 personally and the taxman tops this up with £8,000).

His gross pension contribution is deducted from his taxable income, giving him a threshold income of £185,000. Because Dirk's threshold income is less than £200,000, he is completely unaffected by the tapered annual allowance. This means his annual allowance for the current tax year (his permitted pension contribution) is £40,000.

Example 2

Beric is a company owner and pays himself salary and dividend income totalling £200,000. He also has taxable rental profits of £40,000, so his total taxable income is £240,000.

His company makes a pension contribution of £35,000 for him (an employer contribution) but we ignore this when calculating his threshold income. He doesn't make any pension contributions personally.

Beric's threshold income is therefore £240,000. Because this exceeds £200,000, he is potentially affected by the tapered annual allowance.

Adjusted Income

If your threshold income exceeds £200,000 the next thing you have to calculate is your 'adjusted income'. Broadly speaking, your adjusted income is your total taxable income *plus* any pension contributions made by your employer.

You also add back any contributions to an occupational pension scheme under a net pay arrangement (where your contributions are deducted from your salary before calculating PAYE).

You can also deduct the reliefs listed in Section 24 of the Income Tax Act 2007.

Your annual allowance will only be reduced if your adjusted income exceeds £240,000 (previously £150,000). The annual allowance is reduced by £1 for every £2 your adjusted income exceeds £240,000. So an individual with adjusted income of £270,000 will have their annual allowance reduced by £15,000 (£30,000/2), giving them an annual allowance of £25,000.

The annual allowance cannot fall below £4,000.

Pension contributions that exceed the tapered annual allowance face the annual allowance charge. The excess contributions will be added to your income and taxed. If the charge exceeds £2,000 it may be possible to have it paid out of your pension savings. This may only be possible if total contributions to the scheme in question exceed the standard annual allowance (£40,000).

Example 2 continued

As we saw earlier, Beric has total taxable income of £240,000 and his company makes a contribution of £35,000 on his behalf.

Beric's adjusted income is £275,000 (£240,000 + £35,000)

His annual allowance is cut by (£275,000 - £240,000)/2 = £17,500

His annual allowance is therefore £40,000 - £17,500 = £22,500

Beric faces an annual allowance charge on £12,500:

£35,000 - £22,500 = £12,500

Calculating the Tapered Annual Allowance in Practice

Beric can avoid the charge by getting his company to make a smaller pension contribution (no more than £26,667).

Alternatively, he may be able to extract less income from his company (no more than £175,000) to ensure his total taxable income reduces to £215,000 and he is able to benefit from a tapered annual allowance of £35,000. Company owners may find it easier than others to control their taxable income to reduce their threshold income and adjusted income. But they may have to be wary of triggering a special tax anti-avoidance rule (see below).

Most regular salaried employees will find it fairly easy to calculate their adjusted income and threshold income. So too will company owners who pay themselves a set amount of salary and dividend income. Problems may arise where the taxpayer has income that is less predictable, for example profits from self employment or rental profits from property. In these circumstances it may not be possible to calculate how much taxable income you have (and thus the tapered annual allowance) until *after* the tax year has ended. By then it will be too late to make pension contributions.

Those who wish to benefit from pension contributions and think they are affected by the tapered annual allowance may therefore need to estimate their total taxable income just *before* the end of the tax year.

The Tapered Annual Allowance and Carry Forward

Fortunately, all is not lost if your pension contributions exceed your tapered annual allowance for the year. Those affected by the tapered annual allowance can still carry forward any unused annual allowance from the three previous tax years. For example, if your annual allowance this year is reduced from £40,000 to £30,000 and you make a £20,000 pension contribution, you will have £10,000 left to carry forward to next year (£30,000 - £20,000).

Carry forward could act as a lifeline for those whose pension contributions accidentally exceed the tapered annual allowance in any given year. Beric in the above example will avoid the annual allowance charge if he has at least £12,500 of unused annual allowance from the three previous tax years.

Anti-Avoidance Rule

An anti-avoidance rule is in place to prevent anyone entering into an arrangement which involves reducing their adjusted or threshold income and increasing their income in a different tax year. The anti-avoidance provisions apply when it is reasonable to assume that the main purpose, or one of the main purposes of the arrangement, is to reduce the impact of the tapered annual allowance. If the anti-avoidance provisions apply, then the relevant arrangement will be ignored for the purposes of calculating the tapered annual allowance.

It is unclear how this anti-avoidance rule could be applied to individuals such as company owners who vary their income from year to year.

Maximum Pension Contribution

Thanks to the changes made in 2020 many high earners are now unaffected by the tapered annual allowance and can once again make fairly big pension contributions with full tax relief.

For example, anyone with a taxable income of up to £240,000 can personally contribute up to £40,000 to a pension every year (assuming there are no employer contributions). The following table shows how much high earners can personally contribute at different income levels.

140

Taxable income	Maximum pension contribution*
Up to £240,000	£40,000
£250,000	£35,000
£260,000	£30,000
£270,000	£25,000
£280,000	£20,000
£290,000	£15,000
£300,000	£10,000
£310,000	£5,000
£312,000	£4,000

* Maximum gross contribution that can be paid personally. Assumes there is no employer contribution. Ignores carry forward from 3 previous tax years.

Maximum Contributions – Company Owners

A company owner with taxable income of up to £200,000 can get their company to make a pension contribution of up to £40,000 every year with full tax relief. The following table shows how much the company can contribute at different income levels:

Taxable Income	Maximum Company Pension Contribution*
Up to £200,000	£40,000
£215,000	£35,000
£230,000	£30,000
£245,000	£25,000
£260,000	£20,000
£275,000	£15,000
£290,000	£10,000
£305,000	£5,000
£308,000+	£4,000

* Assumes there is no contribution by the company owner personally. Ignores potential carry forward from 3 previous tax years

Planning under the Tapered Annual Allowance

Some very high income earners may be comfortable with a reduced annual allowance. For example, a sole trader with profits of £260,000, who makes regular pension contributions of £20,000 per year, may be quite happy with an annual allowance of £30,000.

However, if they expect their income to increase, resulting in further reductions in their annual allowance, it may be desirable for them to make bigger pension contributions now while they can. In other words, it may be better to contribute £30,000 now instead of £20,000.

Some individuals whose threshold income is *below* £200,000 at present may also wish to speed up their pension contributions at present if they expect to be earning well over £200,000 in a few years' time.

It may also be possible to mitigate the damage caused by the tapered annual allowance by getting your spouse to make bigger pension contributions, even if these only attract 40% tax relief.

Example
Miriam is a self-employed solicitor with profits of £300,000 and her husband Nick earns £100,000. During the current tax year Miriam would like to make a pension contribution of £40,000 but is restricted to £10,000. Nick normally makes pension contributions of £10,000 per year.

The couple therefore decide to swap the amounts they contribute: Nick contributes £40,000 per year (using the couple's shared resources) and Miriam contributes £10,000.

Nick's additional pension contribution of £30,000 will only attract 40% tax relief, compared with Miriam's 45%, however the total loss of tax relief is just £1,500 (£30,000 x 5%).

For this strategy to work it is essential that Nick has sufficient income taxed at 40% so that all of the additional contribution attracts higher-rate tax relief (see Chapter 4).

It may also be essential that Nick's higher contributions do not result in him building such a big pension pot that his withdrawals, when he eventually retires, are taxed at 40% instead of at the 20% basic rate of income tax.

Part 5

Employees

Chapter 21

Auto-Enrolment: The Advent of Compulsory Pensions

"Currently 14 million people get no contribution from their employer towards a pension."

Former Secretary of State for Work and Pensions, Yvette Cooper, January 2010

To address this problem, compulsory workplace pensions have been phased in over the last few years. Known as 'auto enrolment' it forces all employers to enrol nearly all their staff into a workplace pension.

Exemptions

Only employees earning more than £10,000 and aged from 22 to state pension age need to be *automatically* enrolled into a pension. However, some older and younger employees and those who earn less than £10,000 also have workplace pension rights:

- If an employee earns less than £6,240 in 2022/23 they don't need to be automatically enrolled but the employer has to give them access to a pension if they request it and if they are aged between 16 and 74. However, the employer is not required to contribute.

- If an employee earns between £6,240 and £10,000 and their age is between 16 and 74 they don't need to be automatically enrolled but do have the right to opt in. If they do decide to join the pension scheme the employer will have to contribute as well.

- If an employee earns more than £10,000 but is aged 16-21 or between state pension age and 74 they don't need to be automatically enrolled but do have the right to opt in. If they do decide to join the pension scheme the employer will have to contribute as well.

Company Directors

According to the Pension Regulator a company does not have any automatic-enrolment duties when:

- It has just one director, with no other staff

- It has a number of directors, none of whom has an employment contract, with no other staff

- It has a number of directors, only one of whom has an employment contract, with no other staff

A contract of employment does not have to be in writing. However, according to the Pension Regulator, if there is no written contract of employment, or other evidence of an intention to create an employer/worker relationship between the company and the director, it will not argue that an employment contract exists.

If a director does not have an employment contract they do not need to be assessed for automatic enrolment.

If a director has a contract of employment and is not the only person working for the company under an employment contract, they are not exempt. Depending on their age and earnings, they may then qualify for automatic enrolment.

However, unlike other employees, the company may choose not to enrol a director who qualifies for automatic enrolment. If the company chooses not to enrol the director, the director still has the right to opt in or join a pension.

If the company decides not to enrol an employed director who is eligible for automatic enrolment, and it has no other eligible staff, it does not have to set up a pension scheme.

However, it will need to make a 'declaration of compliance'.

The Contributions

Employers are forced to make a minimum pension contribution and, in practice, so too are most employees.

Generally speaking, contributions are a percentage of 'qualifying earnings'.

The total minimum contribution is 8% with at least 3% coming from the employer.

The total minimum contribution can be paid by the employer but in practice many small firms will insist that the employee makes up the required balance.

This means that many employees are forced to contribute 5% to a pension if they want to benefit from a 3% contribution from their employer.

Employees' contributions enjoy tax relief as normal, which means 4% will come from them personally and the extra 1% will be added by the taxman in the form of basic-rate tax relief.

Qualifying Earnings

The minimum contributions are generally not based on the employee's total earnings but rather on a band of earnings.

The lower and upper thresholds for 2022/23 are £6,240 and £50,270 respectively. What this means is that pension contributions are typically based on earnings of up to £44,030 (£50,270 - £6,240).

For example, someone with employment income of £60,000 will have their pension contributions based on earnings of £44,030. Someone with employment income of £20,000 will have their pension contributions based on earnings of £13,760 (£20,000 - £6,240).

Opting out

Employees will be automatically enrolled but can opt out if they wish by completing an opt-out notice. Employers are, however, required to automatically re-enrol eligible employees back into the workplace pension scheme roughly every three years.

No doubt some employees, especially younger employees, will prefer to opt out if they are compelled by their employers to make a pension contribution of up to 5%.

How Valuable is Auto Enrolment?

The answer to this question probably depends on whether you are an employee or employer.

Many small business owners cannot afford to save for their own retirement, let alone those of their entire workforce!

And this, perhaps, is the crucial point. If your employer has been dragged kicking and screaming into a system of compulsory pensions, you may end up being paid less to cover the cost. For example, future pay increases may be reduced. This is basic economics.

Even an 8% pension contribution is not big enough to solve most people's retirement saving problem, especially since it will typically be based on a small band of the employee's earnings.

For example, let's say you currently earn £65,000 and you and your employer make a combined 8% pension contribution for 20 years (based on the £44,030 band of qualifying earnings), with all amounts increased to take account of inflation.

After 20 years the pension pot will be worth around £180,000, if the investments in the fund grow by, say, 7% per year. That's a tidy sum BUT insignificant in terms of providing you with a meaningful retirement income.

In 20 years' time your salary may have grown to around £95,000, so the money paid into your pension pot will be worth less than two years' salary – not exactly enough for a golden retirement!

This does not mean that you should opt out of auto-enrolment. That would mean forfeiting the pension contribution your employer makes, which could arguably be regarded as free money.

What it does mean is that those who are making the minimum pension contribution under auto enrolment will almost certainly need to build additional retirement savings, either using pensions or other savings products.

Chapter 22

Free Cash from Employers

As we know from the previous chapter, many individuals enjoy more than just tax relief on their pension contributions. They also receive 'free' money from their employers.

Many company pension schemes offer far more generous employer contributions than those required under the auto-enrolment rules. Some employees receive employer contributions totalling 5%-10% of their salary, provided they contribute a similar amount. With the help of employer pension contributions, you may be able to save twice as quickly as you could on your own.

Sometimes employers will double what you put in. For example, in one pension scheme I know about, the company puts in 12% if the employee puts in 6%.

Many employees recognize that giving up any of this free money (by not contributing at all or not contributing enough) is tantamount to looking a gift horse in the mouth.

I remember listening on the radio to a woman describe how she and her husband were trying to cut out every single bit of frivolous spending so that they could contribute as much as possible to her husband's workplace pension scheme, thereby enjoying a hefty matching contribution from the employer.

She described it as "austerity today for prosperity tomorrow".

Not everyone has been as financially prudent as this couple. According to Standard Life, before the advent of auto-enrolment employers were offering a contribution to around 10 million employees but around 4.5 million did not sign up to their employer's pension scheme.

These employees were missing out on a total of nearly £6 billion per year of free money!

Not surprisingly in the past it has been younger employees who have contributed the least to pensions. According to the

Department for Work and Pensions, in 2011 only 15% of employees aged 16-24 participated in workplace pension schemes, whereas pension participation was 58% in the 45-54 age group.

Millions more people now belong to a workplace pension thanks to the introduction of compulsory pensions (see Chapter 21) BUT some employees (e.g. younger employees) may opt out.

I'm not in the business of criticising the savings habits of others, especially those who have children to support. Many families have very little income left after paying extortionate amounts of income tax, national insurance and VAT and after paying down debts like student loans and home mortgages.

Nevertheless, if there is ever a good time to contribute to a pension it's when your employer is offering you money on a plate.

Example
Douglas is an employee with a salary of £60,000 per year. Let's say his employer offers to make a 5% pension contribution, with Douglas contributing 5% personally.

If Douglas decides to opt out of his workplace pension scheme, he will have additional income of £3,000 (£60,000 x 5%). After paying income tax he will be left with £1,800.

Alternatively, if Douglas decides to join his workplace pension scheme he will end up with £6,000 sitting in his pension (£3,000 contributed personally and £3,000 from his employer).

Douglas has to decide whether £1,800 of income today is more valuable than £6,000 tucked away until he retires.

This is just a snapshot from a single year. Douglas will lose £4,200 (£6,000 - £1,800) every year he is not a member of his employer's pension scheme. Furthermore, he will also lose the tax-free growth on that money. If a 25-year-old decides to forego a pension contribution from his employer he will lose possibly 40 years of tax-free compound growth. On next year's foregone contribution he will lose 39 years of tax-free growth... and so on.

So how much do you stand to lose over the long term by not receiving pension contributions from your employer?

Example continued

Let's say Douglas opts out of his workplace pension scheme for five years and therefore loses out on five years of employer contributions (at 5% of his salary).

We'll assume his salary increases by 3% per year, which means the contributions from his employer will also grow by 3% per year. We'll also assume the money in his pension grows by 7% per year tax free.

Douglas loses out on the following employer contributions over the five-year period: £3,000, £3,090, £3,183, £3,278 and £3,377. When you add tax-free compound growth at 7% per year, the total value of the employer pension contributions after five years is £19,523.

However, that's not the end of the story. Depending on how far away Douglas is from retirement he could lose out on tax-free growth on this money for possibly another 10, 20, 30 or even 40 years. For example, those five years' worth of contributions will be worth £27,382 after 10 years, £53,865 after 20 years, £105,960 after 30 years and £208,439 after 40 years.

Remember, all we are looking at here are the contributions that would be made by Douglas's employer (the 'free money'). We are ignoring the contributions that he would make personally and on which he would enjoy full income tax relief.

The top half of Table 6 shows exactly the same thing for a range of different starting salaries. In each case we assume the salary grows by 3% per year, the employer makes a 5% pension contribution for five years and the money grows by 7% per year tax free.

For example, if your salary is £30,000 now and you lose out on five years' worth of employer contributions and an additional 15 years of tax-free growth on that money, the total loss to your pension pot after 20 years will be £26,932.

The second half of the table shows exactly the same thing except this time we assume the employee is not a member of the workplace pension scheme for 10 years. For example, if your salary is £30,000 now and you lose out on 10 years' worth of employer contributions and an additional 10 years of tax-free growth on that money, the total loss to your pension pot after 20 years will be £49,193.

Table 6
5% Employer Pension Contribution
Long-term Value

Employer Contributions for 5 Years
Value after...

Starting Salary £	10 Years £	20 Years £	30 Years £	40 Years £
20,000	9127	17,955	35,320	69,480
30,000	13,691	26,932	52,980	104,220
40,000	18,255	35,910	70,640	138,959
50,000	22,818	44,887	88,300	173,699
60,000	27,382	53,865	105,960	208,439
70,000	31,946	62,842	123,620	243,179
80,000	36,509	71,820	141,280	277,919
90,000	41,073	80,797	158,940	312,659
100,000	45,637	89,774	176,600	347,399

Employer Contributions for 10 Years
Value after...

Starting Salary £	10 Years £	20 Years £	30 Years £	40 Years £
20,000	16,672	32,795	64,514	126,908
30,000	25,007	49,193	96,770	190,362
40,000	33,343	65,591	129,027	253,816
50,000	41,679	81,989	161,284	317,270
60,000	50,015	98,386	193,541	380,724
70,000	58,350	114,784	225,798	444,178
80,000	66,686	131,182	258,054	507,632
90,000	75,022	147,579	290,311	571,086
100,000	83,358	163,977	322,568	634,540

Different Employer Pension Contributions

Different employers pay different amounts into their employees' pensions.

To find out how much a bigger or smaller employer contribution is worth all you have to do is scale the numbers in Table 6 up or down.

For example, if the employer offers a 10% contribution you simply double the numbers. In this case Douglas, with a starting salary of £60,000 and no contributions for five years, will have lost £107,730 after 20 years (£53,865 x 2).

If the employer offers an 8% contribution you multiply the numbers by 1.6 (found by dividing 8 by 5).

If the employer offers a 3% contribution you multiply the numbers by 0.6 (found by dividing 3 by 5).

... and so on.

Putting Things in Perspective

The numbers in the table are quite large and imply that, by not belonging to a workplace pension scheme, and not receiving pension contributions from your employer, you may be losing a lot of free money.

However, it's important to put the figures in perspective. Let's say Douglas is 35 years old and 30 years away from retirement. By not receiving employer pension contributions for five years, his pension pot will have lost £105,960 of free money after 30 years.

However, by that time his salary will have grown to £141,394 (growing at just 3% per year). What this means is that not contributing to his employer's pension for five years has cost him around nine months' salary.

Is this a price worth paying? Only Douglas can answer that.

And what if Douglas is a high flier and his pay increases by more than inflation, as he climbs the corporate ladder?

154

If we assume his salary grows by 7% per year we find that after 30 years he is sitting on a salary of £426,855. And his pension pot will have lost out on £114,184 worth of employer contributions.

In total Douglas will have lost just over three months' pay by not receiving pension contributions from his employer for five years.

Personally, I am of the opinion that anyone offered free cash by their employer should grasp the opportunity with open arms.

BUT...

If you do not belong to your workplace pension scheme for just a few years, this may not have a significant effect on your income in retirement IF you expect your salary to grow rapidly, resulting in bigger employer pension contributions in later years.

Part 6
Salary Sacrifice Pensions

Chapter 23

Introduction to
Salary Sacrifice Pensions

How would you like to increase your pension contributions by up to 34%, with the taxman footing the entire bill? It seems too good to be true but this result can be achieved if you stop making pension contributions *personally* and get your employer to make them all for you.

This set-up is known as salary sacrifice (also salary exchange or 'smart pensions') and is used by some of the country's biggest companies and universities, including BT, Tesco and the BBC.

In my opinion, a salary sacrifice pension is the best tax-saving opportunity available to regular salaried employees.

So how does it work? Salary sacrifice is all about saving *national insurance*, on top of the income tax relief you already receive when you make pension contributions.

Most people only enjoy income tax relief when they contribute to a pension. The income tax relief is attractive but it's not the maximum amount of tax relief available. When an employee contributes personally to a pension plan there is no refund of all the national insurance paid by both the employee and the employer. As much as £258 of national insurance is paid by the employee and employer on £1,000 of salary.

With salary sacrifice it's possible to put a stop to these national insurance payments because your employer makes your pension contributions for you.

Pension contributions paid by employers are exempt from national insurance.

The national insurance savings can then be added to your pension pot.

Sacrificing Salary, Not Income

Because the employer has to pay all the employee's pension contributions, the employee in return has to sacrifice some salary.

However, it's important to stress that the employee's net take-home pay does not fall – it remains exactly the same.

With salary sacrifice there is no extra cost for either the employee or the employer.

Clamp Down on Salary Sacrifice

The Government was concerned about the amount of money lost from salary sacrifice schemes. As a result, the income tax and employer's national insurance advantages of some salary sacrifice schemes have been removed.

However, employer pension contributions are not affected and continue to benefit from income tax and national insurance relief.

However, as with everything in the world of tax, it's possible the Government could change the rules at any time and abolish salary sacrifice pensions too.

Company Pension Scheme Not Required

In theory salary sacrifice works with almost all pension plans including:

- Self-invested personal pensions (SIPPs)
- Personal pensions (group and individual plans)
- Stakeholder pensions (group and individual plans)
- Occupational pension schemes

The main consideration for salary sacrifice purposes is that the plan must be able to accept employer contributions. Many SIPP providers have special forms for this purpose.

However, if a salary sacrifice pension arrangement is used by your employer in conjunction with his auto-enrolment duties, it's essential the pension plan is a "qualifying scheme" for auto-enrolment purposes.

The pension provider will be able to tell you if the scheme is qualifying or not.

Salary sacrifice can be used by most employees. However, sole traders and other self-employed individuals cannot use salary sacrifice because there is no employer to make pension contributions on their behalf.

There has to be an employer/employee relationship for a salary sacrifice arrangement to be successful.

Chapter 24

Income Tax & National Insurance: A Five-Minute Primer

In this chapter I'm going to briefly explain how income tax and national insurance are calculated for the average salary-earning employee. This should make the examples easier to digest.

Furthermore, because national insurance rates and thresholds have been changed so many times this year, all examples use the rates that will apply next year (2023/24) and in future years.

Calculating Income Tax

For the 2023/24 tax year, which starts on 6th April 2023, most employees will pay income tax as follows:

- 0% on the first £12,570 Personal allowance
- 20% on the next £37,700 Basic-rate band
- 40% above £50,270 Higher-rate threshold

If you earn more than £50,270 you are a higher-rate taxpayer; if you earn less you are a basic-rate taxpayer.

Different rates apply in Scotland. The examples in the chapters that follow are based on the rates applying in the rest of the UK.

Example – Basic-Rate Taxpayer

John earns a salary of £25,000. His income tax for 2023/24 can be calculated as follows:

- *0% on the first £12,570 = £0*
- *20% on the next £12,430 = £2,486*

Total income tax bill: £2,486

Example – Higher-Rate Taxpayer

Jane earns a salary of £60,000. Her income tax for 2023/24 can be calculated as follows:

- *0% on the first £12,570 = £0*
- *20% on the next £37,700 = £7,540*
- *40% on the final £9,730 = £3,892*

Total income tax bill: £11,432

Income above £100,000 and £125,140

When your income exceeds £100,000 your tax-free personal allowance is gradually withdrawn and when your income exceeds £125,140 you will start paying tax at 45% (the additional-rate threshold has been reduced from £150,000 to £125,140 from the start of the 2023/24 tax year).

Calculating National Insurance

For the 2023/24 tax year employees will pay national insurance as follows:

- 0%   on the first   £12,570   Primary threshold
- 12%   on the next   £37,700
- 2%   above   £50,270   Upper earnings limit

Employers will generally pay 13.8% national insurance on every single pound the employee earns over £9,100. There is no cap.

You probably don't lose much sleep over your employer's national insurance bill. However, employer's national insurance is a tax on YOUR income. If it didn't exist your employer would be able to pay you a higher salary.

Here are John and Jane's national insurance calculations:

Example – Basic-Rate Taxpayer

John earns a salary of £25,000. His national insurance for 2023/24 can be calculated as follows:

- *0%   on the first   £12,570 = £0*
- *12%   on the next   £12,430 = £1,492*

John's national insurance bill: £1,492

John's employer pays national insurance on John's salary as follows:

- *0%   on the first   £9,100   = £0*
- *13.8% on the next   £15,900   = £2,194*

John's employer's national insurance bill: £2,194

Example – Higher-Rate Taxpayer

Jane earns a salary of £60,000. Her national insurance for 2023/24 can be calculated as follows:

- *0%   on the first   £12,570 = £0*
- *12%   on the next   £37,700 = £4,524*
- *2%   on the final   £9,730   = £195*

Jane's national insurance bill: £4,719

Her employer's national insurance is:

- *0%   on the first   £9,100   = £0*
- *13.8% on the next   £50,900   = £7,024*

Jane's employer's national insurance bill: £7,024

Tax Bills Combined

John and Jane's tax bills can be summarised as follows:

John – Basic-rate Taxpayer – £25,000

	£
Income tax	2,486
Employee's national insurance	1,492
Employer's national insurance	2,194
Total taxes	**6,172**

Jane – Higher-rate Taxpayer – £60,000

	£
Income tax	11,432
Employee's national insurance	4,719
Employer's national insurance	7,024
Total taxes	**23,175**

When you include employer's national insurance it's startling how much tax is paid even by those on relatively modest incomes. Direct taxes on John's income come to 25%.

An amount equal to 39% of Jane's salary is paid in direct taxes.

The Health and Social Care Levy (HSCL)

Under previous proposals, a new 1.25% tax called the Health and Social Care Levy was going to be introduced from 6th April 2023.

This unnecessary complication to the tax system has, we are pleased to say, been scrapped for now.

Chapter 25

Salary Sacrifice Case Study: Basic-Rate Taxpayer

Introduction

We are going to follow the same John from the previous chapter and show how his own pension contributions can be increased by 34% with a salary sacrifice pension. All figures are for 2023/24.

Remember John earns £25,000 and is a basic-rate taxpayer. Employees who are basic-rate taxpayers pay 20% income tax and 12% national insurance.

John's Retirement Savings

John pays income tax of £2,486 and national insurance of £1,492 on his £25,000 salary.

Let's say he also personally contributes £1,000 into his employer's pension scheme.

His employer pays the amount to the pension scheme provider who in turn reclaims £250 of basic-rate tax relief from HMRC and credits this to John's pension pot, bringing his total pension contribution to £1,250.

(The assumption here is that the pension scheme uses the 'relief at source' method rather than the 'net pay' method – see Chapter 2.)

The company John works for also makes an employer contribution into his pension plan. Although this is welcome, we will ignore this contribution and focus on John's own contributions.

After deducting his taxes and pension contribution he is left with a disposable income of £20,022.

Saving National Insurance

This is not a bad outcome but John can do much better. So far he has enjoyed full *income tax* relief on his pension contributions. However, income tax is not the only tax John pays. He also pays 12% national insurance on a significant chunk of his salary and his employer pays 13.8%.

Unfortunately, there is no national insurance relief for pension contributions made personally by employees like John. However, there is full national insurance relief for pension contributions made by employers.

John and his employer therefore agree that John will stop contributing personally to the pension scheme and his employer will make all the contributions for him. In return, John agrees to sacrifice some salary.

John's Salary Sacrifice

John sacrifices £1,471, which takes his salary from £25,000 to £23,529 (I explain why he sacrifices this amount later).

After deducting income tax and national insurance on £23,529 he is still left with £20,022 – the exact amount of disposable income he had before.

John's employer pays the £1,471 of sacrificed salary directly into John's pension plan.

His employer also contributes an additional £203, representing the employer's national insurance saving: £1,471 x 13.8% = £203. The amount going into John's pension pot now is £1,674 (plus his employer's original pre-salary sacrifice contribution).

In summary, John still has £20,022 of take-home pay, just as before, but his pension contribution has increased from £1,250 to £1,674 – an increase of 34%.

He is now saving 20% income tax, 12% employee's national insurance and 13.8% employer's national insurance on the money paid into his pension plan. A summary of the number crunching is contained on the next page.

John's Take Home Pay Stays the Same

	Before Salary Sacrifice	After Salary Sacrifice
	£	£
Salary	25,000	23,529
Less:		
Income tax	2,486	2,192
National insurance	1,492	1,315
Pension contribution	1,000	0
Disposable income	**20,022**	**20,022**

... But His Pension Contribution Increases By 34%

	Before Salary Sacrifice	After Salary Sacrifice
	£	£
Employee contribution	1,000	-
Taxman's top up	250	-
Extra employer contribution	-	1,471
Employer's NI saving paid in	-	203
Total	**1,250**	**1,674**

34% –The Magic Number!

Although this is just a one-year snapshot, what we can deduce from this simple example is that basic-rate taxpayers who use salary sacrifice can boost their pension contributions by 34%.

This means salary sacrifice could have a BIG impact on the amount of money you are able to save for retirement.

For example, if you would expect your own pension contributions to eventually grow in value to £100,000 without salary sacrifice, then you can expect them to grow to £134,000 with salary sacrifice.

If you would expect your own pension contributions to grow in value to £200,000 without salary sacrifice, you can expect them to grow to £268,000 with salary sacrifice … and so on.

These are significant increases. Remember this extra money is completely **free**! You would not have to save a single penny extra to enjoy this boost to your retirement savings.

The extra money comes about because you and your employer are saving national insurance.

Note, your *total* pension pot will not increase by 34%, just the amount that you were originally contributing personally. Remember John's employer was already contributing to his pension before the salary sacrifice took place. His employer's *original* (pre-salary sacrifice) contributions will not increase under a salary sacrifice arrangement.

How to Calculate Your Own Salary Sacrifice

Let's say you are a basic-rate taxpayer and personally contribute £1,000 to a pension. To get that £1,000 you will have had to earn salary of £1,471:

£1,471 *less* 20% income tax *less* 12% national insurance = £1,000

So if you give up £1,471 of salary *and* stop making pension contributions you will still have almost exactly the same amount of disposable income.

Therefore, to calculate how much salary to sacrifice, while keeping your disposable income the same, you simply take your net pension contribution and add back the 20% income tax and 12% national insurance you have paid.

To do this quickly, divide your net pension contribution by 0.68:

$$\frac{\text{Net Pension Contribution}}{0.68}$$

Example 1

John, as we know, is a basic-rate taxpayer and personally contributes £1,000 to his employer's pension plan annually (this is his net pension contribution). His total gross contribution, including the taxman's top up, is £1,250. The amount of salary John needs to sacrifice is:

$$£1,000/0.68 = £1,471$$

If John stops contributing to his pension plan and sacrifices this amount of salary, his disposable income will remain the same.

His employer will contribute £1,471 to his pension plan plus an extra £203 (£1,471 x 13.8%), representing the employer's national insurance saving. His total pension contribution will be £1,674 – an increase of £424 per year or 34%.

Example 2

Richard is a basic-rate taxpayer and personally contributes £3,000 to his employer's pension plan annually (this is his net pension contribution). His total gross contribution, including the taxman's top up, is £3,750. The amount of salary Richard needs to sacrifice is calculated as follows:

$$£3,000/0.68 = £4,412$$

If Richard stops contributing to his pension plan and sacrifices this amount of salary, his disposable income will remain the same.

His employer will contribute £4,412 to his pension plan plus an extra £609 (£4,412 x 13.8%), representing the employer's national insurance saving. His total pension contribution will be £5,021 – an increase of £1,271 per year or 34%.

Chapter 26

Salary Sacrifice Case Study: Higher-Rate Taxpayer

Introduction

In this chapter we are going to follow the same Jane from Chapter 24 and show how she can boost her pension pot with a salary sacrifice arrangement.

Remember, Jane earns £60,000 and is a higher-rate taxpayer. In 2023/24 higher-rate taxpayers will pay 40% income tax and 2% national insurance on their earnings over £50,270.

Jane's Retirement Savings

We know from Chapter 24 that Jane's income tax and national insurance bill comes to £16,151.

Let's say she also personally contributes £2,400 into her employer's pension scheme. Her employer pays the amount to the pension scheme provider who in turn reclaims £600 of basic-rate tax relief from HMRC and credits this to Jane's pension pot, bringing her total pension contribution to £3,000.

Jane also receives a £600 income tax refund when she submits her tax return (her higher-rate tax relief).

(The assumption here is that the pension scheme uses the 'relief at source' method rather than the 'net pay' method – see Chapter 2.)

The company Jane works for also makes an employer contribution into her pension plan. Although this is most welcome, we will ignore this contribution and focus on Jane's own contributions.

After deducting her taxes and pension contribution and adding back her higher-rate tax relief, Jane is left with disposable income of £42,049: £60,000 - £16,151 - £2,400 + £600.

Saving National Insurance

So far Jane has enjoyed full *income tax* relief on her pension contributions but no national insurance relief because, as we know, there is no national insurance relief for pension contributions made by employees.

So Jane decides to stop contributing personally and asks her employer to make the contributions directly. In return, Jane agrees to sacrifice £3,103 of salary which takes her from £60,000 to £56,897 – I'll explain why she sacrifices this exact amount shortly.

After deducting income tax and national insurance she is left with £42,049 – the exact amount of disposable income she had before.

Jane's employer pays the £3,103 of sacrificed salary directly into her pension plan. Her employer also contributes the employer's national insurance saving, which comes to £428 (£3,103 x 13.8%).

Jane's pension contribution is now £3,531 and has increased by 18%.

It's not as much as the 34% increase enjoyed by John, the basic-rate taxpayer, because higher-rate taxpayers generally only save 2% national insurance on the salary they sacrifice, whereas basic-rate taxpayers save 12%.

Both types of taxpayer, however, can benefit from their employers' 13.8% national insurance saving.

It is also important to remember that Jane is enjoying much more *income tax* relief than John (40% as opposed to 20%).

In summary, Jane is enjoying 40% income tax relief, 2% employee's national insurance relief and 13.8% employer's national insurance relief on the money she contributes to her pension plan.

A summary of the number crunching is contained on the next page.

Jane's Take Home Pay Stays the Same

	Before Salary Sacrifice	After Salary Sacrifice
	£	£
Salary	60,000	56,897
Less:		
Income tax	10,832*	10,191
National insurance	4,719	4,657
Pension contribution	2,400	0
Disposable income	**42,049**	**42,049**

... But Her Pension Contribution Increases By 18%

	Before Salary Sacrifice	After Salary Sacrifice
	£	£
Employee contribution	2,400	-
Taxman's top up	600	-
Extra employer contribution	-	3,103
Employer's NI saving	-	428
Total	**3,000**	**3,531**

* Reduced by £600 higher-rate income tax relief.

18% –The Magic Number!

Although this is just a one-year snapshot, what we can deduce from this simple example is that higher-rate taxpayers who use salary sacrifice can boost their pension contributions by 18%.

This means salary sacrifice could have a significant impact on the amount of money you are able to save for retirement.

For example, if you would expect your own pension contributions to eventually grow in value to £100,000 without salary sacrifice, then you can expect them to grow to £118,000 with salary sacrifice.

If you would expect your own pension contributions to grow in value to £200,000 without salary sacrifice, then you can expect them to grow to £236,000 with salary sacrifice ... and so on.

These are significant increases. Remember this extra money is completely **free**! You would not have to save a single penny extra to enjoy this boost to your retirement savings.

The extra money comes about because you and your employer are saving national insurance.

Note, your *total* pension pot will not increase by 18%, just the amount that you were originally contributing personally. Remember Jane's employer was already contributing to her pension before the salary sacrifice took place. Her employer's *original* (pre-salary sacrifice) contributions will not increase under a salary sacrifice arrangement.

How to Calculate Your Own Salary Sacrifice

Let's say you are a higher-rate taxpayer and personally contribute £1,000 to your pension. The gross contribution is £1,250 (£1,000/0.8) and you will receive £250 of higher-rate relief (£1,250 x 20%). So the actual cost to you is just £750 (£1,000 - £250).

To get £750 of income in your hands you will have had to earn £1,293 of salary:

£1,293 _less_ 40% income tax _less_ 2% national insurance = £750

So if you sacrifice £1,293 of salary and stop making pension contributions you will still have the same amount of disposable income to spend.

To perform the same calculation for yourself and calculate how much salary you need to sacrifice just follow these two simple steps:

- **Step 1.** Multiply the amount you personally contribute to your pension by 0.75 – the resulting number is what your pension contributions are actually costing you and takes into account your higher-rate relief.

- **Step 2.** Add back the 40% income tax and 2% national insurance you have paid on this income. To do this divide the result from Step 1 by 0.58:

$$\frac{\text{Step 1}}{0.58}$$

Example

As we know, Jane is a higher-rate taxpayer and personally contributes £2,400 to her pension. The taxman tops this up with £600, so her gross pension contribution is £3,000. Jane's salary sacrifice is calculated as follows:

- **Step 1.** Multiply the amount she personally contributes to her pension by 0.75:

$$£2,400 \times 0.75 = £1,800$$

- **Step 2.** Add back her 40% income tax and 2% national insurance by dividing the result by 0.58:

$$£1,800/0.58 = £3,103$$

If she sacrifices £3,103 of salary and stops contributing to her pension plan, her disposable income will remain the same.

Her employer will contribute £3,103 to her pension plan, plus an extra £428 (£3,103 x 13.8%). This is the employer's national insurance saving. Her total pension contribution will now be £3,531.

It's important to remember that she can enjoy this free increase to her pension pot **every year.**

Furthermore, this is just her national insurance saving. As a higher-rate taxpayer she will also be enjoying 40% income tax relief on her pension contributions.

A higher-rate taxpayer who personally contributes £2,400 to a pension plan will receive a £600 income tax refund from the taxman so the actual cost is just £1,800. The taxman's top-up will take the total pension contribution to £3,000.

With salary sacrifice the pension contribution then goes up to £3,531 without costing a penny extra.

Chapter 27

How to Convince Your Employer

After over 20 years in the tax publishing business one thing I have learnt is that most tax breaks come with a catch.

With salary sacrifice pensions the catch is you need your employer's co-operation. If your employer isn't already offering a salary sacrifice arrangement, you'll have to get them to agree to it and to do the necessary paperwork (see Chapter 29).

How much bargaining power you have with your employer will, of course, depend on how big the company is and how senior you are.

If you are a senior executive at a small or medium-sized company, you should find it relatively easy to get your employer to introduce a salary sacrifice arrangement. If you are a junior employee at a multinational corporation your chances are probably slim.

However, because a salary sacrifice arrangement could increase your pension pot by thousands of pounds, I believe it's worth fighting for tooth and nail.

Fortunately, there are several arguments you can use to convince your employer:

Argument #1 Other Employers Are Doing It

Salary sacrifice pensions are available from some of the country's biggest and most reputable companies, universities and other organisations, including BT, Tesco and the BBC.

To stay competitive in the jobs market your employer should also be offering this benefit.

Argument #2 Easy to Implement

As we will see in Chapter 29, the paperwork is relatively straightforward and may only have to be done once. Having said this, some employers may shy away from introducing a salary sacrifice arrangement if they are grappling with their auto-enrolment duties and if they fear that a salary sacrifice pension arrangement will not be auto-enrolment compliant.

Argument #3 Giving Employees a FREE Pay Increase

This is by far the most powerful argument you can use to convince your employer to introduce a salary sacrifice pension arrangement.

The employee effectively receives a pay increase that doesn't cost the employer anything. The taxman foots the entire bill.

What rational employer would turn down such an opportunity?

Sharing the Savings with Your Employer

If you are struggling to convince your employer to introduce a salary sacrifice pension arrangement, you can offer to share the national insurance savings.

Remember there are two types of national insurance: the type the employee pays and the type the employer pays.

In all the examples so far we have assumed that both the employee's and employer's national insurance savings are paid into the employee's pension plan.

However, to convince your employer to introduce a salary sacrifice pension arrangement you may have to appeal to his selfish side and offer to share the national insurance savings.

Your employer generally pays 13.8% national insurance on every pound you earn over £9,100. It may be necessary to offer your employer, say, half of the employer's national insurance saving (6.9% of the salary sacrifice amount) to co-operate with you.

Ideally you should negotiate to have your employer share the national insurance savings for just one year, perhaps to compensate them for time spent doing the necessary paperwork. However, even if your employer insists on a permanent national insurance share, you will still be far better off in most cases with a salary sacrifice pension arrangement.

For example, in Chapter 25 we showed how John, a basic-rate taxpayer, saw his pension contribution go up from £1,250 to £1,674 with a salary sacrifice arrangement – an increase of 34%. This was helped by his employer contributing the full national insurance saving of £203.

If his employer had only agreed to contribute half his saving, John's pension contribution would have increased from £1,250 to £1,573 – an increase of 26%. John is still significantly better off with a salary sacrifice pension.

Similarly, in Chapter 26 we showed how Jane, a higher-rate taxpayer, saw her pension contribution go up from £3,000 to £3,531 with a salary sacrifice arrangement – an increase of 18%. This was helped by her employer contributing the full national insurance saving of £428.

If her employer had only agreed to contribute half the saving Jane's pension contribution would have increased from £3,000 to £3,317 – an increase of 11%. Jane is still better off with a salary sacrifice pension.

Employer Refuses to Share NI Savings

What happens if your employer refuses to share any of the national insurance savings? This is the worst-case scenario but cannot be ruled out.

If you are a basic-rate taxpayer a salary sacrifice pension may still be worth having because your pension contributions will still be approximately 18% higher.

If you are a higher-rate taxpayer, however, a salary sacrifice pension will increase your pension contributions by a paltry 3%. Remember, higher-rate taxpayers only pay 2% national insurance on earnings over £50,270. So a salary sacrifice saves them very little unless some or all of the employer's much larger 13.8% national insurance bill is also added to the pension pot.

In summary, a salary sacrifice arrangement loses most of its attractiveness if you are a higher-rate taxpayer and your employer refuses to share the national insurance savings.

When Your Employer Doesn't Pay NI

Most businesses currently receive an allowance of £5,000 per year to offset against their national insurance bills. Thus in some small companies – those employing just a few people on low salaries – there may be no employer's national insurance payable.

There's also no employer's national insurance on salary income under the higher-rate threshold (£50,270) paid to under 21s and apprentices under 25.

If the business doesn't have any national insurance to pay, a salary sacrifice will not produce an employer's national insurance saving that can be paid into the employees' pensions.

Summary

- Salary sacrifice requires your employer's approval.

- To convince your employer to introduce salary sacrifice you can use the following arguments:

    - Many big, reputable employers offer salary sacrifice
    - It is relatively easy to implement
    - It allows employers to provide FREE pay increases

- The national insurance savings can be shared with your employer. A basic-rate taxpayer could still end up with a 26% bigger pension pot. A higher-rate taxpayer could still end up with an 11% bigger pension pot.

- If your employer refuses to share any of the national insurance savings, a salary sacrifice arrangement is still worthwhile if you are a basic-rate taxpayer... but much less attractive if you are a higher-rate taxpayer.

Chapter 28

Salary Sacrifice Drawbacks

With salary sacrifice your gross salary is reduced, so anything that depends on your gross salary could be affected, including your:

- Employment benefits
- Borrowing ability
- Maternity pay

For starters, the general consensus among pension experts is that you should not take part in a salary sacrifice arrangement if your income will fall below the lower earnings limit (currently £6,396).

This is because your entitlement to various state benefits may be affected if your income falls below the lower earnings limit, including state pension, statutory sick pay, and maternity pay.

Also, your employer cannot let a salary sacrifice take you under the national minimum wage or national living wage.

Employment Benefits

If a salary sacrifice reduces your gross salary then this could *potentially* also reduce your:

- Future pay increases
- Overtime
- Life insurance cover provided by your employer
- Redundancy payments

Many salary sacrifice arrangements address this issue by making sure all benefits are based on the employee's original salary – often referred to as the reference salary, notional salary or base salary. So if you are currently earning £40,000 and your salary is reduced to £37,000, your employment benefits can be calculated on the basis that you are still earning £40,000.

Borrowing Ability

Any salary reduction could affect your ability to borrow money, for example to buy a house or for any other purpose.

One solution is for your employer to provide the lender with a letter of reference confirming your reference salary. For example, some of the university salary sacrifice documents state that:

"You should quote your current annual salary on mortgage applications and your payslip will substantiate this figure as your annual salary. If The University Payroll Office receives requests for mortgage references from lenders they will quote your current salary i.e. before the reduction."

This potential issue can therefore be addressed. However, there is still a potential risk that some lenders will not accept your reference salary and use the lower post-sacrifice salary.

New State Pension

Since 2016 the basic state pension and state second pension have been replaced with a flat-rate pension worth £203.85 per week – £10,600 per year in 2023/24.

Nowadays your state pension entitlement is based solely on how many years of national insurance contributions or credits you have – the amount you earn is irrelevant.

Under the previous system your entitlement to the state second pension was based on your earnings and could therefore have been adversely affected by a salary sacrifice.

To qualify for the new state pension you need 35 years of national insurance contributions or credits – five years more than before. If you have less than 35 years you will get a proportion of the full state pension. For example, if you have 28 years of contributions you will get 80%.

To qualify for any state pension you will need a minimum level of contributions, usually 10 years worth. If you have less than this you will not receive any pension.

Maternity Pay

A salary sacrifice arrangement could reduce the amount of statutory maternity pay (SMP) to which you are entitled. Statutory maternity pay is based on your contractual earnings which count for national insurance contributions. So if your earnings have been reduced because you sacrificed some salary, the amount of statutory maternity pay you receive may also be reduced.

If a salary sacrifice takes your salary below the lower earnings limit (currently £6,396), you will lose your statutory maternity pay entitlement altogether.

How is Statutory Maternity Pay Calculated?

Women are entitled to 52 weeks of maternity leave and 39 weeks of statutory maternity pay.

For the first six weeks you are entitled to receive 90% of your average gross weekly earnings, with no upper limit. So a salary sacrifice could reduce the amount of SMP you receive for the first six weeks.

For the remaining 33 weeks you are entitled to receive the *lesser* of:

- £172.48 per week (2023/24)
- 90% of your average weekly earnings

All except the lowest paid will receive a flat amount of £172.48 per week for this 33-week period, so a salary sacrifice will probably have no effect on this part of your SMP entitlement.

Statutory Maternity Pay – Effect on the Employer

Employers are liable to pay statutory maternity pay but can get most of it refunded.

If the employer's total payments of class 1 national insurance are £45,000 or less the employer can recover 103% of the SMP paid.

The extra amount is to compensate for the employer's national insurance payable on the SMP.

If the employer's total class 1 national insurance payments are more than £45,000 per year, the employer can recover 92% of the SMP paid.

Employer vs Employee

With salary sacrifice pensions the idea is that neither the employee nor the employer ends up worse off. However, salary sacrifice pension arrangements could prove costly for employers when their staff are on parental leave.

The general rule is that employer pension contributions must continue to be made as normal while an employee is on paid parental leave. With salary sacrifice the employer's pension contributions are larger than normal so the cost could be higher.

Maternity Allowance

Maternity allowance is paid to women who are employed but not entitled to SMP. Maternity allowance is based on your earnings, so a salary sacrifice arrangement may reduce your entitlement to maternity allowance.

Chapter 29

How to Implement a Salary Sacrifice Pension

It is important to point out that salary sacrifice must be a *contractual agreement*, not an informal arrangement between you and your employer.

In other words, you have to change your employment contract and this should to be done in writing.

It may be possible to change your contract of employment by using a simple agreement letter, signed by both you and your employer. Many pension companies provide sample documents. This letter should be kept with your employment contract.

The new agreement must state what benefit is being received in exchange for the sacrificed salary.

It's important that the potential future salary is given up before it is treated as received for tax and national insurance purposes. Your terms of employment must be changed *before* the salary sacrifice commences.

HMRC is not against salary sacrifice but could challenge the arrangement if it has not been set up correctly and the paperwork is not in order.

Salary Sacrifice and Auto Enrolment

The operation of a salary sacrifice arrangement is separate from the automatic enrolment provisions (see Chapter 21), although the Pension Regulator states that employers can run the two in parallel when complying with their employer duties.

An employer can ask an employee who must be automatically enrolled whether they want to use a salary sacrifice arrangement. However, active membership of a pension scheme cannot depend on the employee agreeing to use salary sacrifice. If the employee does not agree to salary sacrifice, the employer must automatically enrol them into the pension scheme with an alternative method of making pension contributions.

The qualifying earnings used to work out the minimum pension contribution required under auto-enrolment are based on the post-sacrifice level of salary.

However, some commentators argue that it is better to base contributions on the pre-sacrificed salary to maintain good relations with employees.

Getting HMRC Approval

HM Revenue & Customs does not have to be notified of salary sacrifice arrangements. However, after the arrangement is set up employers can ask HMRC to advise on the tax and national insurance consequences.

This gives the employer reassurance the arrangement has been implemented correctly.

HMRC will probably want to see evidence that the employment contracts have been changed correctly and payslips, before and after the sacrifice.

For more information:

www.gov.uk/guidance/non-statutory-clearance-service-guidance

Payslips and P60s

Strictly speaking, your new post-salary-sacrifice payslip should not show your old salary, with the sacrificed amount shown as a deduction.

However, HMRC's guidance notes state that if the employment contract has been changed correctly, the payslip is less important.

However, if there are issues surrounding the employment contract, the payslip may be used to determine whether the salary sacrifice is valid.

186

HMRC recognises that some payroll software can only store one value for the employee's salary. This could create problems when calculating overtime and other benefits based on the higher pre-sacrifice reference salary.

However, as long as the contract has been modified correctly, and makes it clear that the employee is entitled to a reduced salary and specified benefits, HMRC should not invalidate the salary sacrifice.

HMRC's guidance notes point out that non-taxable benefits-in-kind must not be carried forward to the P60.

Finally, I would strongly recommend speaking to an advisor who has experience of salary sacrifice pensions and auto-enrolment before diving in and setting one up yourself.

Part 7

Company Directors

Chapter 30

Introduction

Company directors, just like regular employees, can contribute up to 100% of their 'relevant UK earnings' to a pension and receive full tax relief but typically not more than £40,000 (the annual allowance).

Your relevant UK earnings will include your:

- Salary and any bonus
- Taxable benefits in kind

For example, a company director with a salary of £20,000 can make a cash contribution of up to £16,000. The taxman will top this up with £4,000 of basic-rate tax relief for a gross pension contribution of £20,000.

A company director whose only income is a salary of £60,000 can make a cash contribution of up to £32,000. The taxman will top this up with £8,000 of basic-rate tax relief for a gross pension contribution of £40,000. He can make an additional pension contribution of £20,000 gross if he has unused annual allowance from any of the previous three tax years.

(Of course, as we saw in Chapter 4, the director may not want to make such a large contribution in practice because he would not receive higher-rate tax relief on the whole contribution.)

Company Pension Contributions

As a company owner you can also get your company (your employer) to make pension contributions on your behalf. Company pension contributions are always paid *gross* (there is no top up from the taxman) but the company will normally enjoy corporation tax relief on the payment.

For example, a company currently paying 19% corporation tax and making a pension contribution of £10,000 will receive corporation tax relief of £1,900 (£10,000 x 19%).

Pension contributions made by employers are not restricted by the level of the employee's earnings. A company pension contribution can be bigger than the director's earnings. However, there are other restrictions on company pension contributions.

Firstly, total pension contributions by you and your company must not exceed the £40,000 annual allowance, although any unused allowance from the previous three tax years can be carried forward and used to cover contributions made by both you and the company. (High income earners may be subject to a lower annual allowance – see Chapter 20.)

Secondly, the company may be denied corporation tax relief on any pension contributions made on behalf of directors, if the taxman views them as 'excessive'. We'll return to this point later.

In this part of the guide we explain why pension contributions are an attractive alternative to dividends.

We also answer the important question asked by many company owners: "Who should make the pension contributions: me or the company?"

However, before doing that it's important to explain how company owners often structure their pay to reduce income tax.

Chapter 31

Salary or Dividend?

Most small company owners are both directors and shareholders. This means they can withdraw both salaries and dividends from their companies. Salaries are subject to income tax and national insurance, dividends are subject to income tax only.

Taking a big salary is usually very expensive because of the national insurance cost. This year up to 12.73% national insurance will have to be paid by the company owner personally and an extra 14.53% will usually have to be paid by the company.

But extracting all the profits as dividends is not the best solution either for most small company owners because this means subjecting all of the company's profits to corporation tax (dividends are paid out of after-tax profits).

The optimal solution in many cases is to take a small salary that is tax deductible in the company's hands and mostly free from national insurance in the hands of the director.

"Optimal" Salaries for 2022/23

There are three important thresholds for the 2022/23 tax year:

- Employer's national insurance   £9,100
- Employee's national insurance   £11,908
- Income tax   £12,570

For many company owners taking a salary equal to one of the above three thresholds is optimal.

A salary of £11,908 will be tax efficient for many directors who don't have any taxable income from other sources in 2022/23.

There will not be any employee's national insurance and, providing the company owner has no other income, will also be free from income tax. A small amount of *employer's* national insurance will be payable, compared with a completely tax-free salary of £9,100, but the corporation tax relief on the extra payment usually outweighs the national insurance cost.

A salary of £11,908 will not be optimal for everyone. For example, where the company owner has taxable income from other sources, a small tax saving may be achieved by taking a salary of £9,100 instead of £11,908.

If your company doesn't use up its £5,000 national insurance employment allowance paying salaries to other employees, there may be spare employment allowance for the directors own salaries. In this case a salary of up to £12,570 may be more tax efficient (or cost very little extra in tax). However, in some cases sticking with a salary of £11,908 may be more tax efficient, for example when the company owner has income from other sources.

Note that the employment allowance is not available to companies where a single director is the sole employee. According to HMRC guidance, the employment allowance also cannot be claimed if there are other employees BUT the director's salary is the only one on which employer's national insurance is payable.

What has all this got to do with pensions? If you get your company to pay you a small salary because it is tax efficient to do so, you can only make a small pension contribution personally. This is because, to enjoy tax relief, your pension contributions cannot exceed your earnings. However, your *company* can make pension contributions on your behalf and these will not be restricted by your small salary.

There are many tax and non-tax factors that may influence your salary decision. Some company owners may prefer a bigger salary because, although strictly speaking not "optimal", this lets them take a bigger chunk of income out of the company on a regular basis, without some of the hassle that comes with paying dividends (for example, making sure the company has sufficient distributable profits and that dividends are properly declared).

For a complete discussion of this topic see the Taxcafe guide *Salary versus Dividends*.

How Dividends Are Taxed

Once they've paid themselves a small salary, many company owners take the rest of their income as dividends.

Dividends are subject to income tax but not national insurance. The income tax rates on dividends are lower than the income tax rates on salaries because dividends are paid out of a company's *after-tax* profits: the money has already been taxed in the company's hands, whereas salaries are a tax deductible expense.

The first £2,000 of dividend income you receive in 2022/23 is tax free thanks to the dividend allowance. The dividend allowance is to be cut to £1,000 in 2023/24 and then to just £500 in 2024/25.

The income tax rates on dividend income were increased significantly in 2016 and by a further 1.25% on 6th April 2022. For those receiving dividends in excess of the dividend allowance, the following tax rates apply (old rates included for comparison):

	Old rates	Current rates
Basic-rate taxpayers	7.5%	8.75%
Higher-rate taxpayers	32.5%	33.75%
Additional-rate taxpayers	38.1%	39.35%

Because income paid as dividends is taxed twice (first in the hands of the company and second in the hands of the shareholder) it's easy to lose sight of how much tax is being paid overall. As a company owner you are possibly just as concerned about your company's tax bill as your own, so it's worth showing the overall combined tax rates on dividend income.

For a company that has paid 19% corporation tax, the total tax rates on dividend income are now as follows:

	Total Tax Rate (rounded)
Basic-rate taxpayers	26%
Higher-rate taxpayers	46%
Additional-rate taxpayers	51%

If the company has £100 of profit it will pay £19 corporation tax, leaving £81 to pay as dividends. Ignoring the £2,000 dividend allowance, a higher-rate taxpayer will pay £27 tax on this income (£81 x 33.75%), so the total tax on the £100 profit is £46, i.e. 46%.

The above tax rates are a fair bit higher than the "regular" income tax rates that apply to most types of income (20% for basic-rate taxpayers, 40% for higher-rate taxpayers and 45% for additional-rate taxpayers).

This is because the Government has been trying to level the playing field between company owners (who often pay little or no national insurance because they take most of their income as dividends) and self-employed business owners and regular employees, who pay national insurance on most of their earnings.

From a tax planning perspective, once they've used up their £2,000 dividend allowance, company owners may be better off paying themselves income that is taxed at the regular income tax rates in preference to dividends, where possible. Examples include interest and rental income (but not salary income if both income tax and national insurance are payable).

Corporation Tax Increase

From 1st April 2023 the main rate of corporation tax will be increased from 19% to 25%.

The corporation tax increase will affect company profits as follows:

- **Profits £50,000 or less** – Company will continue to pay 19% tax on all of its profits

- **Profits between £50,000 and £250,000** – Company will pay 19% tax on the first £50,000 and 26.5% on the remainder

- **Profits greater than £250,000** – Company will pay 25% tax on all of its profits

As a result, the combined tax rates on dividend income will also naturally increase for many company owners.

For example, where a company has profits greater than £250,000 and pays 25% tax on all of its profits, the total tax rates on dividend income will be:

	Total Tax Rate
Basic-rate taxpayers	31.56%
Higher-rate taxpayers	50.31%
Additional-rate taxpayers	54.51%

The corporation tax increase will thus make it even more attractive for company owners to pay themselves certain other types of income that are taxed at the "regular" tax rates (for example, interest income and rental income) in preference to dividends.

As a result of the corporation tax increase many companies will also enjoy more tax relief on pension contributions they make for their directors and employees, as we shall see in the next chapter.

A Final Word on Company Owners and their Pay

Finally, please note that I am not recommending that company owners structure their pay in the way described in this chapter. You should always speak to an accountant about your own optimal pay structure.

Chapter 32

Pension Contributions: Better than Dividends?

Following the latest increase in dividend tax rates in April 2022, some company owners may be thinking about paying themselves smaller dividends and getting their companies to make bigger pension contributions instead.

When their company's corporation tax rate increases, some company owners may find it even more appealing to make pension contributions instead of paying themselves additional dividend income. This is because dividends will be paid out of profits that have been more heavily taxed.

By contrast, when the corporation tax rate increases many companies will enjoy more tax relief on any pension contributions they make for their directors and employees.

At the time of writing many companies are enjoying 19% tax relief on their pension contributions but this will rise to 26.5% for those with profits between £50,000 and £250,000 and 25% for companies with profits in excess of £250,000.

If such a company has profits of £100,000 it will currently save £1,900 corporation tax by making a pension contribution of £10,000. When the company's marginal rate of tax increases to 26.5% it will save £2,650 tax.

There are several reasons why pension contributions are currently an attractive alternative to dividends and may become even more attractive when corporation tax increases:

- Like salaries, company pension contributions enjoy corporation tax relief. In other words, they're a tax deductible business expense.

- Unlike salaries, there is no national insurance on the income you eventually withdraw from your pension.

- When you eventually withdraw money from your pension, 25% can be taken tax free.

- Pension income is taxed at the 'regular' income tax rates, typically 20% or 40%. By contrast, for companies currently paying 19% corporation tax, the combined tax rate on dividend income is around 26% for basic-rate taxpayers and 46% for higher-rate taxpayers. When corporation tax increases these combined tax rates will rise to approximately 32% and 50% respectively for owners of companies with profits in excess of £250,000. Similar rates will be payable by many owners of smaller companies.

- When you start withdrawing income from your pension, you could find yourself in a lower tax bracket than you are now (many retirees are basic-rate taxpayers). This means you could end up paying income tax at just 20%.

Putting all this together, it's possible that you could ultimately pay income tax on your pension withdrawals at an overall effective rate of just 15%.

By contrast, you may face a combined tax rate that is possibly two to three times higher if the same money is paid out as dividend income.

There is, of course, a major drawback with pensions: your money is locked away until you are 55 (rising to 57 in 2028). Nevertheless, when you do reach the minimum retirement age you can make unlimited withdrawals.

Another drawback with pensions is you are potentially exposed to any future increase in income tax rates. Essentially your savings are at the mercy of future governments.

Having said this, we do believe that pension contributions are still worth making in many cases.

Example – Higher-rate Taxpayer
Before Corporation Tax Increase

Lesleyanne is a company owner and a higher-rate taxpayer (i.e. her taxable income is more than £50,270).

Let's say she is trying to choose between taking an additional £1,000 of the company's profit as a dividend and getting the company to invest £1,000 in her self-invested personal pension (SIPP).

With a dividend the company will first pay corporation tax at 19% (£190), leaving £810 to distribute. Lesleyanne will then pay income tax at 33.75%: £273. The total combined tax rate on the dividend is roughly 46%.

By contrast, a company pension contribution will enjoy corporation tax relief so the whole £1,000 will go straight into Lesleyanne's SIPP. Ignoring investment growth (it doesn't affect the outcome), when she eventually withdraws the money from her pension the first £250 will be tax free and the remaining £750 will be subject to income tax.

If Lesleyanne is a basic-rate taxpayer when she retires in the future she will pay 20% income tax (£150), leaving her with £850 overall. Thus her effective overall tax rate will be 15%.

If Lesleyanne is a higher-rate taxpayer when she retires (for example, if she ends up with a significant amount of rental income from buy-to-let properties) she will effectively pay 40% tax on her taxable pension income (£300), leaving her with £700 overall. Thus the effective tax rate on her pension withdrawals will be 30%.

If Lesleyanne does not have much income from other sources when she retires (except perhaps for her state pension), it's also possible that some of her pension withdrawals will be covered by her income tax personal allowance and therefore tax free. Although this is a distinct possibility for many retirees we will ignore it for the remainder of this chapter so as not to overstate the potential benefits of pensions.

In summary, Lesleyanne's choice is between paying tax at roughly 46% on her additional dividend income and paying tax at 15% or possibly 30% on her pension withdrawals.

Example – Higher-rate Taxpayer
After Corporation Tax Increase

Let's say that after the increase in corporation tax is in full force Lesleyanne's company makes profits of approximately £100,000 and she is once again trying to choose between the same additional dividend and pension contribution.

With a dividend the company will face a marginal corporation tax rate of 26.5% which means it will pay £265 tax, leaving £735 to distribute. Lesleyanne will then pay income tax at 33.75%: £248. The total combined tax rate on the dividend will be roughly 51%.

With a company pension contribution the whole £1,000 will go straight into Lesleyanne's SIPP. The effective tax rate on her pension withdrawals will be either 15% if she is a basic-rate taxpayer when she retires or 30% as a higher-rate taxpayer.

In summary, Lesleyanne's choice will be between paying tax at roughly 51% on her additional dividend income and paying tax at 15% or possibly 30% on her pension withdrawals.

What these examples show is that, for company owners who have not yet built up significant pension savings, a company pension contribution is currently an extremely attractive alternative to additional dividend income and will become even more attractive when the corporation tax increase is in full force.

Of course, one must never lose sight of the fact that your pension savings are placed in a locked box until you are at least 55. So a company pension contribution is only an attractive alternative to a dividend if you have already withdrawn enough money from your company to cover your living costs.

In the above example we have assumed that the company will have a marginal tax rate of 26.5% after the increase in corporation tax. If its profits are greater than £250,000 it will face a marginal tax rate of 25%. In this case Lesleyanne's choice will be between paying tax at roughly 50% on her additional dividend income and paying tax at 15% or possibly 30% on her pension withdrawals.

Are company pension contributions attractive if you're a basic-rate taxpayer (i.e. if your taxable income is less than £50,270)? Let's find out:

Example – Basic-rate Taxpayer
Before Corporation Tax Increase

Poppy is a company owner and a basic-rate taxpayer. She too is trying to choose between taking £1,000 of the company's profit as a dividend and a £1,000 company pension contribution.

With a dividend the company will first pay corporation tax at 19% (£190), leaving £810 to distribute. Poppy will pay income tax at 8.75%: £71. The total combined tax rate on the dividend is roughly 26%.

With a company pension contribution the whole £1,000 will go straight into Poppy's SIPP. As with Lesleyanne, the effective tax rate on her pension withdrawals will be either 15% if she is a basic-rate taxpayer when she retires or 30% if she is a higher-rate taxpayer.

In summary, Poppy's choice is between paying tax at roughly 26% on her additional dividend income and paying tax at 15% or possibly 30% on her pension withdrawals.

Example – Basic-rate Taxpayer
After Corporation Tax Increase

If the company's profits do not exceed £50,000 in the future it will continue to pay corporation tax at 19% and the outcome will be the same as the above example.

With a dividend, if the company has profits in the £50,000-£250,000 bracket it will face a marginal corporation tax rate of 26.5% which means it will pay £265 tax on the £1,000 of profit, leaving £735 to distribute. Poppy will then pay income tax at 8.75%: £64. The total combined tax rate on the dividend will be roughly 33%.

In summary, Poppy's choice will be between paying tax at roughly 33% on her additional dividend income and paying tax at 15% or possibly 30% on her pension withdrawals.

What this example shows is that, if you are a basic-rate taxpayer, a company pension contribution is currently a reasonably attractive alternative to additional dividend income and will become even more attractive when corporation tax increases. However, pension contributions will not be very attractive if Poppy ends up wealthier in retirement and becomes a higher-rate taxpayer. This could happen if, for example, she inherits or accumulates a significant amount of assets and the income takes her over the higher-rate threshold before she starts withdrawing money from her pension.

Periods Straddling the Date of Change

The above examples all use the 19% corporation tax rate that currently applies to many companies or rates that will apply after the increase is in full force.

However, we also have to consider those rates that apply to accounting periods that straddle 1st April 2023, the date the corporation tax rate increases. Some companies are already in this situation and are therefore already partly affected by the corporation tax increase, others will be soon. Pension contributions in these years will potentially enjoy more than 19% tax relief but not quite as much as when the corporation tax increase applies for the whole year.

Example 1

Three Trees Ltd has an accounting period that runs from 1st August to 31st July and has taxable profits of approximately £200,000 per year. The company faces the following marginal corporation tax rates:

- *August 2021 to July 2022   19%*
- *August 2022 to July 2023   21.51%*
- *August 2023 to July 2024   26.5%*

If the company made any pension contributions before 31st July 2022 it will have enjoyed 19% tax relief. Any contributions it makes between 1st August 2022 and 31st July 2023 will enjoy up to 21.51% tax relief. Any contributions made from 1st August 2023 onwards will enjoy up to 26.5% tax relief.

Example 2

Four Firs Ltd has an accounting period that runs from 1st January to 31st December and has taxable profits of approximately £200,000 per year. The company faces the following marginal corporation tax rates:

- *Year ended 31st December 2022   19%*
- *Year ended 31st December 2023   24.65%*
- *Year ended 31st December 2024   26.5%*

If the company makes pension contributions before 31st December 2022 it will enjoy 19% tax relief. Any contributions between 1st January 2023 and 31st December 2023 will enjoy up to 24.65% tax relief. Any contributions made from 1st January 2024 onwards will enjoy up to 26.5% tax relief.

(See the Taxcafe guide *The Company Tax Changes* for a full discussion of how marginal corporation tax rates are calculated.)

Postponing Pension Contributions

Some may be wondering whether it is worth postponing or reducing pension contributions until their company's corporation tax rate increases, so that more tax relief can be enjoyed.

(Note, here we are talking about voluntary pension contributions, typically for the directors, rather than compulsory ones due under auto-enrolment.)

A company with profits of £50,000-£250,000 will eventually face a marginal rate of 26.5% and may be able to enjoy £75 of additional tax relief for every £1,000 of pension contributions it postpones. A company with profits of more than £250,000 may be able enjoy up to £60 of additional tax relief.

It's certainly worth considering postponing contributions but it should be pointed out that this strategy is not without its risks and practical problems.

For starters, the company may have to wait quite some time to enjoy the maximum tax relief. Take a company with accounting periods that run from January to December. Only pension contributions made from January 2024 onwards will enjoy up to 26.5% tax relief, although contributions made between January and December 2023 will enjoy up to 24.65% tax relief.

Some company owners may be willing to postpone making contributions until these dates; others may prefer to make more steady contributions.

One reason why it may be worth making pension contributions sooner rather than later is that cash kept inside a company is arguably more vulnerable to commercial risk than cash stored away in a pension.

Another reason is that it is possible that changes could be made to the pension contribution rules that make it harder to make bigger catch-up contributions. For example, at present the annual allowance is £40,000 which means your company can make contributions of up to £40,000 per year on your behalf. It's also possible to make use of any unused annual allowance from the three previous tax years.

But what if the annual allowance is reduced to, say, £20,000 or less? That could make it more difficult for some company owners to receive catch-up contributions.

Furthermore, rumours are always circulating that tax relief on pension contributions will be reduced at some point in the future. We don't know if these rumours have any substance and how any changes would affect company pension contributions.

In summary, postponing or partly reducing pension contributions may produce greater tax savings but you will have to keep your eyes open for changes to pension tax relief that may scupper your plans.

Chapter 33

Pension Contributions: You or the Company?

In the previous chapter we showed that company pension contributions can be an attractive alternative to dividends. However, company directors can also make pension contributions *personally*, so a key question is: *"Who should make the contributions: the director or the company?"*

Company Owner Pension Contributions

When you make pension contributions *personally* (as opposed to getting your company to make them) the taxman will top up your savings by paying cash directly into your pension. For every £80 you invest the taxman will put in an extra £20.

Why £20? Your contributions are treated as having been paid out of income that has already been taxed at 20%, the basic rate of income tax.

The company that manages your pension plan – usually an insurance company or SIPP provider – will claim this money for you from the taxman and credit it to your account.

So whatever contribution you make personally, divide it by 0.80 and you'll get the total amount that is invested in your pension pot (your gross pension contribution).

Example
Peter is a company owner who takes most of his income as dividends. He invests £800 in a self-invested personal pension (SIPP). The taxman will top up his pension with £200 of basic-rate tax relief which means he'll have £1,000 in his pension pot: £800/0.80 = £1,000.

If Peter is a higher-rate taxpayer he can also claim higher-rate tax relief when he completes his tax return. This is given by increasing his basic-rate band by the amount of his gross pension contribution.

Example continued

Peter's gross pension contribution is £1,000 so his basic-rate band will be increased by £1,000. This means £1,000 of his dividend income will be taxed at 8.75% instead of 33.75%, i.e. a 25% saving. Thus, Peter's higher-rate tax relief is: £1,000 x 25% = £250.

In total Peter will enjoy £450 of tax relief (£200 basic-rate relief plus £250 higher-rate tax relief). Peter's total tax relief is 45% of his £1,000 gross pension contribution.

Company Directors with Small Salaries

To obtain tax relief on your pension contributions they have to stay within certain limits:

- **Earnings.** Contributions made by you *personally* must not exceed the greater of £3,600 (gross), or your 'relevant UK earnings'. Earnings include your salary, bonus and taxable benefits in kind but do NOT include your dividends.

- **The £40,000 Annual Allowance.** Total pension contributions by you and your company must not exceed £40,000 per year, although it is possible to carry forward any unused annual allowance from the three previous tax years. The annual allowance is reduced if your 'adjusted income' exceeds £240,000 (see Chapter 20).

For a company director taking a salary of, say, £9,100 (see Chapter 31) the maximum personal pension contribution that can be made with tax relief in 2022/23 is therefore £9,100.

This is the maximum *gross* contribution. The director would personally invest £7,280 (£9,100 x 80%) and the taxman will top this up with £1,820 of basic-rate tax relief for a total gross contribution of £9,100.

For a company director taking a salary of, say, £11,908, the maximum gross pension contribution is £11,908. The director would personally invest £9,526 (£11,908 x 80%) and the taxman will top this up with £2,382 of basic-rate tax relief for a total gross contribution of £11,908.

Directors who want to make bigger pension contributions personally have to pay themselves bigger salaries. However, this may not be an attractive option because a bigger salary may be subject to employer's national insurance (at 14.53% this year) or employee's national insurance (at 12.73%) or both.

Company Pension Contributions

As a company owner you can also get your company (your employer) to make pension contributions on your behalf. Company pension contributions are always paid *gross* (there is no top up from the taxman) but the company will normally enjoy corporation tax relief on the payment. For example, a company currently paying 19% corporation tax can make a pension contribution of £10,000 and enjoy £1,900 tax relief.

Note, you do not need a dedicated company pension scheme to make company pension contributions. Most firms that offer SIPPs allow your company to pay directly into your pension (although these plans may not be qualifying schemes for auto-enrolment purposes).

How much can your company contribute? Unlike the contributions that you make personally, the company's contributions are NOT restricted by the size of your salary.

In other words, the company can make a pension contribution that is bigger than your salary. However, there are other restrictions on company contributions:

- Total pension contributions by you and your company must not exceed the annual allowance (typically £40,000) although you can carry forward any unused allowance from the previous three tax years.

- The company may be denied corporation tax relief on any pension contributions made on behalf of directors, if the taxman views them as 'excessive' (see below).

Corporation Tax Relief on Pension Contributions

Unlike the pension contributions that you make personally, tax relief for company pension contributions is not automatic. Company contributions will only be a tax deductible expense for corporation tax purposes if they are incurred wholly and exclusively for the purposes of the business.

There is a danger that HMRC will deny corporation tax relief for 'excessive' pension contributions. In practice this is relatively rare.

To determine whether company contributions qualify for corporation tax relief, HMRC will look at the total remuneration package of the director. The total package (including salary, pension contributions and other benefits) must not be excessive relative to the work carried out and his or her responsibilities.

Relevant factors may include:
- The number of hours you work, your experience and your level of responsibility in the company.
- The pay of unconnected employees in your company and other companies who perform duties of similar value.
- The pay required to recruit someone to take over your duties.
- The company's financial performance.

Extra care may be necessary in the event of a large one-off company pension contribution.

It may be sensible to document the commercial justification (for example, strong recent financial performance of the company) in the minutes of a directors' board meeting and hold a shareholders' meeting to approve the contribution.

In some cases, when a company is making pension contributions on behalf of all employees, including directors, of more than £500,000 in total, it may be necessary to spread tax relief for the excess over a number of years. These spreading rules will obviously not affect most small companies.

Although the risk that your company will be denied corporation tax relief may be small, it is important to stress that, when it comes to company pension contributions, unlike contributions made by individuals, there is no cast-iron guarantee that the company will enjoy tax relief.

That's why we would recommend speaking to a tax adviser before your company starts making significant contributions.

Pension Contributions: You or the Company?

Using a couple of case studies we will now compare company pension contributions with pension contributions made personally by company owners to see which is most tax efficient.

Case Study 1 – Basic-rate Taxpayer

Eva owns Cassidy Ltd. She is a basic-rate taxpayer and pays herself a salary of £11,908 this year (2022/23) and takes the rest of her income as dividends.

She also decides to use £1,000 of the company's pre-tax profit to fund a pension contribution. If Cassidy Ltd makes the contribution it can pay £1,000 directly into Eva's SIPP and the amount will be a tax deductible expense.

Alternatively Eva can pay herself a dividend to fund a pension contribution she makes personally. We'll assume the company currently pays 19% corporation tax on the £1,000 profit leaving Eva with £810 to take as dividend income.

Eva holds onto £10 and invests £800 in her SIPP. The taxman will add £200 of basic-rate tax relief, leaving her with the same amount in her pension – £1,000.

But that's not the end of the matter: Eva will still have to pay 8.75% tax on her £810 dividend – roughly £70.

Eva is worse off by £60: £70 less the £10 of saved dividend income.

Thus, if you're a basic-rate taxpayer, for every £1,000 that ends up in your pension you may have to pay an additional 6% in tax. In this case a company pension contribution is clearly more tax efficient than a contribution made personally by the director.

Other Important Points

If Eva wants more than £11,908 invested in her pension, making the contribution personally will be even more expensive.

She would have to pay herself a bigger salary and this could result in a significant amount of national insurance becoming payable. This is because, to enjoy tax relief, any pension contribution you make personally cannot exceed the greater of £3,600 (gross) or your earnings (i.e. salary).

The additional salary would typically attract 12.73% employee's national insurance and 14.53% employer's national insurance (unless the company has spare employment allowance).

Case Study 2 – Higher-rate Taxpayer

This time we'll assume Eva is a *higher-rate taxpayer* and again wants to make a £1,000 pension contribution.

If Cassidy Ltd makes the contribution it can pay £1,000 directly into Eva's SIPP. Alternatively Eva can pay herself an £810 dividend, hold onto £10 and invest £800 in her SIPP. The taxman will add £200 of basic-rate tax relief, resulting in the same gross pension contribution of £1,000.

Again, that's not the end of the matter. Eva still has to pay income tax on the additional dividend.

With a gross pension contribution of £1,000, Eva's basic-rate band will be increased by £1,000. This means the £810 dividend will be taxed at just 8.75%, not 33.75%, so the tax is roughly £70.

Furthermore, an additional £190 of her other dividend income will also be taxed at 8.75% instead of 33.75%, saving her an extra £48.

All in all, a £1,000 pension contribution made by the director is £12 more expensive than a contribution made by the company:

£70 income tax - £48 extra relief - £10 saved dividend = £12

In this case a company pension contribution is again more tax efficient than a contribution made personally by the director but the difference is small. Because the saving is so small it will probably be other factors that determine whether the company or the individual makes the pension contribution.

Other Important Points

Note that if Eva wants to enjoy full higher-rate tax relief on a gross pension contribution of £11,908 (i.e. equal to her salary), she must have at least £11,908 of dividend income above the higher-rate threshold (income of at least £62,178 in 2022/23).

If Eva wants to make a pension contribution bigger than £11,908 personally she will have to take a bigger salary and this may result in a significant amount of national insurance becoming payable.

When Personal Contributions Are Attractive

Making pension contributions personally is still worth considering in some situations. Take the example of a director who unexpectedly finds themselves with income of £120,000, which means most of their personal allowance will be withdrawn.

Let's also say the director has received a salary of £9,100 this year. If they make a gross pension contribution of £9,100 they will enjoy full income tax relief on the contribution. Furthermore, their adjusted net income will fall by £9,100 which means £4,550 of their personal allowance will be clawed back, saving them even more tax.

Potentially, the saving in this scenario could be as much as £4,323, reducing the cost of their net £7,280 contribution to just £2,957. That's over £9,000 in your pension at a cost of less than £3,000!

Lifetime ISA versus Company Pension Contribution

In Chapter 15 we examined the Lifetime ISA. Like pensions they attract a top up from the Government but, unlike pensions, ALL the money you take out will be tax free.

Let's say a company owner who is a basic-rate taxpayer is trying to decide between a £1,000 company pension contribution and using a dividend to fund a Lifetime ISA contribution.

A £1,000 pension contribution will attract corporation tax relief so the whole £1,000 will go directly into the company owner's pension.

If the same money is used to pay a dividend to fund a Lifetime ISA contribution, and assuming the company currently pays 19% corporation tax, £810 will be left to pay out. After paying 8.75% income tax the company owner will be left with around £739 to invest in a Lifetime ISA. Adding the Government bonus the company owner will end up with £924 in the Lifetime ISA.

When the company owner reaches age 60, all withdrawals from the Lifetime ISA will be tax free, whereas only 25% of the money withdrawn from the pension will be tax free (although they can get it slightly earlier). The rest will possibly be taxed at just 20% if they are a basic-rate taxpayer.

If we ignore investment growth to keep the example simple (it doesn't affect the outcome), with a Lifetime ISA the company owner will end up with £924; with a pension they will end up with just £850 after tax.

Thus, if you're a basic-rate taxpayer, your retirement income could be 9% higher with a Lifetime ISA

What about higher-rate taxpayers? Once again a £1,000 pension contribution will attract corporation tax relief so the whole £1,000 will go directly into the company owner's pension.

If the same money is used to pay a dividend to fund a Lifetime ISA contribution, and assuming the company currently pays 19% corporation tax, £810 will be left to pay out. After paying 33.75% income tax the company owner will be left with £537 to invest in their Lifetime ISA. Adding the Government bonus the company owner will end up with £671 in their Lifetime ISA.

When the company owner reaches age 60, all withdrawals from the Lifetime ISA will be tax free, whereas only 25% of the money withdrawn from the pension will be tax free. The rest could be taxed at just 20% if they are a basic-rate taxpayer at that point (most retirees currently end up as basic-rate taxpayers).

Ignoring investment growth again, with a Lifetime ISA the company owner will end up with £671; with a pension they will end up with £850 after tax.

Thus, your retirement income could be 27% higher with a <u>pension</u>.

However, if the company owner is a higher-rate taxpayer when they retire (e.g. if they have a lot of income from other sources, such as rental property) they will end up with £700 from a pension, compared with £671 from a Lifetime ISA. The difference is small, so the investment decision will probably be based on other factors in this scenario.

Finally, it's also important to remember that you can only invest £4,000 per year in a Lifetime ISA (with an additional £1,000 bonus from the Government), compared with the maximum gross pension contribution of £40,000 per year. Furthermore, you can only open a Lifetime ISA if you're under 40 years of age and it's only possible to continue making contributions up to age 50.

After the Rise in Corporation Tax

Company pension contributions will become even more attractive as companies become subject to higher corporation tax. Some companies are already in this situation and are partly affected by the corporation tax increase. Let's look at another couple of case studies to see why.

Case Study 3 – Basic-rate Taxpayer

During the 2024/25 tax year Eva has £1,000 of pre-tax profit in Cassidy Ltd that she would like to use to fund a pension contribution. We'll assume Cassidy's marginal tax rate is 26.5%.

If Cassidy Ltd makes the contribution it can pay £1,000 directly into Eva's SIPP.

Alternatively, Eva can use that same £1,000 to pay herself a dividend to fund a pension contribution that she makes personally. The company will pay 26.5% corporation tax leaving the company £735 to pay out as a dividend.

Eva will also have to pay income tax of £64 on the dividend (at 8.75%), leaving her with around £670 to invest in her pension. The taxman will add £168 of basic-rate tax relief (at 20%), resulting in a total gross pension contribution of £838.

In summary, Eva's pension contribution will be over 16% smaller if she decides to make it personally.

Case Study 4 – Higher-rate Taxpayer

This time we'll assume Eva is a *higher-rate taxpayer* and again has £1,000 of pre-tax profit in Cassidy Ltd that she would like to use to fund a pension contribution.

If Cassidy Ltd makes the contribution it can pay £1,000 directly into Eva's SIPP. Alternatively Eva can pay herself a £735 dividend and invest it in her SIPP. The taxman will add £184 of basic-rate tax relief, resulting in a gross pension contribution of £919.

With a gross pension contribution of £919, Eva's basic-rate band will be increased by £919. This means the £735 dividend will be taxed at just 8.75%, not 33.75%, so the tax will be roughly £64. Furthermore, an additional £184 of her other dividend income (£919 less £735) will also be taxed at 8.75% instead of 33.75%, providing additional tax relief of £46.

All in all, Eva will end up with 8% less money in her pension if she decides to make the contribution personally and she will pay an additional £18 of income tax on her £735 dividend.

£64 income tax - £46 extra higher-rate relief = £18

Lifetime ISA versus Company Pension Contribution After the Rise in Corporation Tax

Let's say a company owner who is a basic-rate taxpayer and whose company has a marginal tax rate of 26.5% is trying to decide between a £1,000 company pension contribution and using a dividend to fund a Lifetime ISA contribution.

A £1,000 pension contribution will attract corporation tax relief so the whole £1,000 will go directly into the company owner's pension. When the company owner retires he or she could end up with £850 after tax (first 25% tax free, remainder taxed at 20%).

If the same money is used to pay a dividend to fund a Lifetime ISA contribution, the company will pay 26.5% corporation tax leaving £735 to pay out. After paying 8.75% income tax the company owner will be left with £671 to invest in a Lifetime ISA. Adding the Government bonus the company owner will end up with £839 in the Lifetime ISA, all of which can eventually be withdrawn tax free.

Thus, if you're a basic-rate taxpayer, a company pension contribution could leave you around 1% better off than a Lifetime ISA.

Because the difference is so small the investment decision will probably be based on other factors.

What about higher-rate taxpayers? Once again a £1,000 pension contribution will attract corporation tax relief so the whole £1,000 will go directly into the company owner's pension.

When the company owner retires they could end up with £850 after tax if they are a basic-rate taxpayer at that time (first 25% tax free, remainder taxed at 20%). If they are a higher-rate taxpayer they could end up with £700 (first 25% tax free, remainder taxed at 40%).

If the same £1,000 is used to pay a dividend to fund a Lifetime ISA contribution, the company will pay 26.5% corporation tax leaving £735 to pay out.

After paying 33.75% income tax the company owner will be left with £487 to invest in their Lifetime ISA. Adding the Government bonus the company owner will end up with £609 in their Lifetime ISA, all of which can be withdrawn tax free.

Thus, if you're a basic-rate taxpayer when you retire your retirement income could be 40% higher with a pension.

If you're a higher-rate taxpayer when you retire, your retirement income could be 15% higher.

Summary

- Company pension contributions are currently more tax efficient than contributions made personally by directors.

- The additional saving is currently quite small if the director is a higher-rate taxpayer.

- If you want to make a pension contribution bigger than your existing company salary it is usually more tax efficient to get the company to make the contribution, rather than pay yourself a bigger salary which may have a significant national insurance cost.

- The increase in corporation tax will, in many cases, make company contributions even more attractive than contributions made personally.

- Tax relief for company pension contributions is not automatic – tax relief could be denied if the contributions are viewed as excessive, although this is rare in practice.

- A Lifetime ISA is currently a fairly attractive alternative to a company pension contribution if you are a basic-rate taxpayer. Company pension contributions may be a more attractive alternative if you are a higher-rate taxpayer.

- When corporation tax increases, Lifetime ISAs and company pension contributions may produce a similar outcome if you are a basic-rate taxpayer. Company pension contributions may become even more attractive for many higher-rate taxpayers.

Chapter 34

Taking a Loan from Your Small Self-Administered Scheme (SSAS)

In Chapter 37 we will see how your pension savings can be used to buy commercial property.

This isn't the only way your pension savings can be used to help your business.

Your pension pot can also be used to make a loan to your company.

To do this you will probably have to set up a "small self-administered scheme" (SSAS).

A SSAS is a type of occupational pension scheme, typically established by the owner-managers of a small company (the "sponsoring employer").

SSAS Basics

Although a self-invested personal pension (SIPP) can be used to buy commercial property, a SIPP cannot be used to make a loan to your company.

In theory all pension schemes can make loans to *third parties* but loans to members (or those connected to members) are generally not allowed.

Loans to the sponsoring employers of occupational pension schemes are an exception. A SSAS is an occupational scheme and can therefore lend money to the company that sets it up.

A loan cannot be made to the individual members of the pension scheme or their close relatives or other companies controlled by the members (unless those companies are sponsoring employers of the pension scheme too).

A pension loan can be used for a variety of reasons, for example to buy equipment or stock for the business. However, it cannot be used to a keep a failing company afloat or to directly benefit the members.

A SSAS will typically have no more than 11 members and each member will be a "member trustee" with power over how the money is invested. This exempts the SSAS from certain aspects of the pensions legislation, giving it more flexibility.

Small self-administered schemes are offered by a number of specialist pension companies. They provide all the documentation to establish the SSAS, register it with HMRC, act as the "professional trustee" and manage the day-to-day administration.

Setting up and running a SSAS is more expensive than a conventional SIPP so there's no point using one unless you need the extra flexibility.

For example, one well-known pension company I looked at charges £1,250 to set up a SSAS plus a minimum annual fee of £960. A fee of at least £980 is levied to arrange a loan from the pension scheme, plus at least £240 per year to monitor the loan repayments.

There are also quite a few additional one-off and ongoing charges, including setting up the pension scheme's bank account and handling various aspects of its administration. Some of these fees are fixed, others are levied on a time cost basis (something which always makes me nervous).

Further fees may also be incurred when taking out a loan from the pension scheme, for example obtaining a professional valuation for the assets used as security.

Costs vary from pension company to pension company. You can find out what's on offer by simply doing internet searches using phrases that include "SSAS".

Fees can be paid by the sponsoring company rather than the pension scheme.

Pension Loans – The Rules

Borrowing money from your pension may be a lot more attractive than borrowing from a bank or other conventional lender.

However, it's important to note that your pension scheme cannot give your company a soft loan with no interest payable and flexible repayment terms.

There are several rules that have to be obeyed to avoid so-called "unauthorised payment" tax charges:

Interest Rate

The minimum interest rate that must be charged is set out in HMRC's Prescribed Interest Rates for Authorised Employer Loans.

The interest rate must be *at least* 1% higher than the average of the base lending rates of six big UK banks: Bank of Scotland, Barclays, HSBC, Lloyds, Natwest and RBS.

The average rate is rounded up to the nearest 0.25%.

The current minimum interest rate that must be used can be found on HMRC's website under "Interest charged on underpaid quarterly instalment payments":

https://tinyurl.com/emploanrates

The current minimum interest rate is 4%.

Higher interest rates can be charged and some of the case studies on the pension companies' websites use interest rates closer to 10%.

The point is that, even if a high rate of interest is charged, at least "it's all kept in the family": the interest payments go from *your* company to *your* pension scheme.

The interest payments will be a tax deductible business expense for the company and tax-free income for the pension scheme (because pension schemes don't pay tax on their investment income).

Security

The loan has to be secured by means of a first charge over assets with a value equal to the loan plus all the interest payable on the loan.

The company may be prevented from taking a pension loan if it already has a "floating charge" over its assets.

Some pension administrators insist that the security must be in the form of land or bricks and mortar property.

Other pension companies accept security in the form of intellectual property owned by the company (for example its trademark, customer database etc).

The asset does not have to be owned by the company.

Whatever asset is used it will have to be independently valued, which will result in additional professional fees being incurred.

Using residential property as security is heavily frowned upon by many pension commentators because pension schemes are prohibited from owning residential property in most circumstances.

If the company were to default on the loan, enforcement by the pension scheme of its charge over the property could result in it acquiring a further interest in the taxable property, which will result in unauthorised payment tax charges.

Many pension companies will not allow residential property to be used as security.

Maximum Loan

The loan must not exceed 50% of the net asset value of the pension scheme. So you cannot lend all your pension savings to your company.

Any excess above 50% is treated as an unauthorised payment.

This calculation is performed when the loan is taken out. It doesn't matter if the pension scheme's assets fall in value thereafter.

Length of Loan

The maximum term of the loan is five years. The loan can be rolled over once for another five years in certain circumstances if the company is in genuine financial difficulty.

Repaying the Loan

The loan must be repaid in equal instalments of capital and interest, with at least one payment per year.

If payments fall short an unauthorised payment is deemed to have been made by the pension scheme.

The trustees must take any action necessary to ensure that the loan is repaid, even if this means forcing the company into liquidation.

Unauthorised Payments

If the above rules are broken this could result in an unauthorised payment from the pension scheme.

Unauthorised payments are subject to prohibitive tax charges:

- Unauthorised payment charge – 40% payable by the company

- Scheme sanction charge – 15% payable by the pension scheme administrator (40% if the unauthorised payment charge has not been paid)

- Unauthorised payment surcharge – 15% payable by the company if the unauthorised payments exceed 25% of the value of the pension scheme.

Are Pension Loans a Good Idea?

So is it a good idea to get your company to borrow money from your pension?

One danger is you could end up putting most of your eggs into one basket. If your business goes belly up, you could end up losing a big chunk of your retirement savings as well.

For the same reason it could be argued that business owners should never borrow against their homes.

These three major assets – your business, your pension and your home – should, where possible, be kept completely separate.

This may be a bit unrealistic in practice, however. Borrowing money from a bank is often just as risky for the company owners themselves because banks will usually insist on personal guarantees, typically putting the family home at risk.

In any case why shouldn't an experienced business owner tap their pension pot for a loan if the money will be invested prudently in their business?

Although borrowing from your pension may be acceptable in certain circumstances, I think it would be bordering on insanity to transfer out of a final salary scheme for this purpose.

Are Pension Loans Tax Efficient?

Earlier it was mentioned that, if your company borrows money from your pension scheme, the interest payments will be a tax deductible business expense for the company and tax-free income for the pension scheme.

Does this mean that borrowing money from your pension is tax efficient? Not really. If your company borrowed money from a bank the interest payments would also be tax deductible expense. And the money left in your pension scheme could be invested somewhere else and the investment returns would also be tax free.

However, borrowing from your pension could be less costly overall.

Example – Borrowing from Pension

Jacinda's company, Kiwi Holidays Ltd, needs £100,000 to buy some new equipment.

Jacinda has £200,000 of pension savings, recently transferred into a SSAS.

Let's say Kiwi Holidays borrows £100,000 from the pension scheme and pays 5% interest. For simplicity's sake we will assume the loan is for just one year. The company uses its sales income to repay the loan.

One year later, after the loan is repaid, Jacinda's pension pot will have an additional £5,000 of tax-free interest.

Jacinda's company will have paid out £5,000 interest, with corporation tax relief available on the full amount.

The company will also have paid out £100,000 repaying the initial loan amount but will have £100,000 more equipment.

Example – Borrowing from a Bank

The facts are exactly the same except this time Jacinda's company borrows from a bank instead of her pension.

Let's say Kiwi Holidays pays 5% interest on the bank loan and her pension savings earn 5% interest when invested elsewhere.

One year later Jacinda's pension pot will have an additional £5,000 of tax-free interest, just as in the above example.

Jacinda's company will have paid out £5,000 interest, with corporation tax relief available on the full amount, just as in the above example.

And just as in the above example, the company will have paid out £100,000 repaying the initial loan amount but will have £100,000 more equipment.

In summary, from a *tax* perspective, borrowing from your pension is exactly the same as borrowing from a bank.

However, Jacinda may end up better off overall if the bank charges her company more interest than she can earn on her pension investments.

Example Revised – Borrowing from Bank

Let's say Kiwi Holidays pays 10% interest on the bank loan and her pension savings earn just 5% interest when invested elsewhere.

One year later Jacinda's pension pot will have an additional £5,000 of tax-free interest, just as in the above examples.

But Jacinda's company will have paid out £10,000 interest to the bank. Tax relief can, of course, be claimed on this interest, just as in the previous examples.

The company will also pay out £100,000 repaying the initial loan amount but will have £100,000 more equipment, just as in the above examples.

Jacinda's company ends up with £5,000 less cash by borrowing from a bank (although around £1,000 of this will be recovered in additional corporation tax relief).

So it would appear that company owners are better off borrowing from their pensions if the interest rate charged by a third party lender is higher than the return that can be earned on the pension scheme's investments.

When comparing bank borrowing with pension scheme borrowing it's important to take account of all the costs. As we saw earlier, setting up and running a SSAS, and making arrangements to take a loan, will result in a variety of fees and charges.

Borrowing from the Company Owners

A company can also borrow money from the *company owners* themselves.

The company owners can charge the company interest and, as in all the above examples, the company will be able to claim corporation tax relief on the interest payments, as long as the interest rate charged is not unreasonable.

The company owner is not obliged to charge the company interest, although this is often advisable.

The interest payments from the company will be taxable income in the hands of the company owner. However, it's possible to receive up to £6,000 of tax-free interest income every year thanks to the personal savings allowance and starting rate band.

The personal savings allowance allows you to earn up to £1,000 of tax-free interest if you are a basic-rate taxpayer and £500 if you are a higher-rate taxpayer (nothing if you are an additional-rate taxpayer).

The starting rate band allows you to earn up to £5,000 of tax-free interest. It can only be used by company owners who have less than £5,000 of taxable *non-savings income* (typically salary income and rental income but not dividends).

The £5,000 starting rate band can usually only be enjoyed by company owners who take a small salary (typically no more than the £12,570 personal allowance) and have little or no rental income or other non-savings income.

It's also important to point out that both the £1,000 savings allowance and £5,000 starting rate band eat up your basic-rate band. They are not stand alone allowances. The practical effect is that, if your company pays you £6,000 of tax-free interest, it's possible that £6,000 of your dividend income will be pushed over the higher-rate threshold where it will be taxed at 33.75% instead of 8.75%.

Borrowing to Lend to Your Company

If a company owner doesn't have spare savings to lend to the company they can borrow the money personally and lend it to their company.

Within certain fairly generous limits, the company owner can then claim tax relief for the interest paid to the bank against all of their taxable income (including their interest income or dividend income).

226

Summary

In summary, if a company owner sets up a small self-administered scheme (SSAS) they can use some of their pension savings to make a loan to their company.

This may be attractive if obtaining a conventional bank loan would be difficult or expensive.

There are costs involved when setting up and running a SSAS and arranging a loan.

There are also strict rules that have to be followed, although a reputable pension company will make sure these are all followed to the letter.

Part 8

The Self Employed & Property Investors

Chapter 35

Pension Planning for the Self Employed

The number of self-employed business owners saving for retirement has fallen dramatically in recent years.

Back in the 1990s around 60% were contributing to a pension. Today the figure is closer to 18%.

When HMRC uses the term 'self employed' they are referring specifically to owners of unincorporated businesses, ie sole traders and partnerships. Most company owners are classified as employees (see Part 7 for more on company owners).

Most of the chapters in this guide are relevant for self-employed individuals. However, there are a few additional points that need to be made.

In particular, to maximise the tax relief on your pension contributions it is important to know how much taxable income you have. Most regular employees know how much taxable income they have: all they have to do is look at their payslips.

Many company owners also know how much taxable income they earn *personally*. The *company's* profits may fluctuate from year to year but many directors know how much salary or dividend income they are going to withdraw.

The taxable income of self-employed business owners is often much harder to predict. Taxable income for these individuals is normally the pre-tax profits of the business and there could be significant swings from year to year.

For example, a big order before the end of the tax year could increase taxable profits significantly. Several months of poor trading conditions could see profits fall sharply or even produce a loss for the year.

Sometimes it's not just the sales of the business that will result in big changes to taxable income. The business owner may deliberately drive down taxable profits, for example by making investments in tax-deductible equipment (e.g. vans or computers).

So what has all this got to do with maximising tax relief on pension contributions?

In Chapter 2 we pointed out that to enjoy any tax relief on your pension contributions you must have 'relevant UK earnings'. If your business makes a loss you won't have any earnings and the maximum pension contribution you can make is £3,600 (the 'universal pension contribution' that everyone under age 75 can make).

In Chapter 4 we pointed out that to maximise your higher-rate tax relief, your gross pension contributions should not exceed the amount of income you have over the higher-rate threshold (£50,270 in most parts of the UK, £43,662 in Scotland).

In other words, someone living in England with taxable income of £60,000, who wants to maximise their higher-rate tax relief, should make a gross pension contribution of no more than £9,730 (£60,000 – £50,270).

A sole trader with bumper profits of £90,000 may wish to make a big catch-up pension contribution of almost £40,000 but suspend contributions if taxable profits fall below the higher-rate threshold.

In Chapter 17 we discussed the pros and cons of postponing pension contributions if you are a temporary basic-rate taxpayer. For example, during tough economic times (or if the business has a lot of tax-deductible expenditure for the year) the business owner may become a basic-rate taxpayer and decide to postpone making pension contributions until he or she becomes a higher-rate taxpayer in a future tax year.

Finally, in Chapter 19 we explained why self-employed business owners, who are the highest earners in households that receive child benefit, may wish to make bigger than normal pension contributions when their profits are £50,270 to £60,000. This will help them to reduce or avoid the child benefit tax charge and enjoy higher-rate tax relief.

Calculating Pre-tax Profits

Although many sole traders may wish to vary the amount they contribute to a pension each year in order to maximise their tax relief, the problem for some is they don't know how much profit the business is making.

They may only have this information after they draw up their accounts for the year. This could be many months after the tax year has ended – when it's too late to make pension contributions (you cannot make backdated pension contributions).

Example
Elliott is a sole trader with a 31st March year end.

On 5th April 2023 (the final day of the 2022/23 tax year) he makes a net cash pension contribution of £4,000. The taxman adds £1,000 of basic-rate tax relief to produce a gross pension contribution of £5,000. Elliott expects to have pre-tax profits of over £55,270 for 2022/23 and therefore expects to receive the maximum higher-rate tax relief of £1,000 (£5,000 x 20%).

Elliott's accountant finishes drawing up the accounts for the business in July 2023 and, after taking account of all of his tax-deductible expenditure, calculates that Elliott has pre-tax profits of just £52,000.

This means Elliott will only enjoy higher-rate tax relief on £1,730 of his £5,000 gross pension contribution (£52,000 - £50,270 higher-rate threshold), saving him just £346 in higher-rate tax (£1,730 x 20%). If Elliott had known his profits would be lower than expected, he may have held onto some of his cash and made a bigger pension contribution in a future tax year when his income was higher.

The problem for Elliott is he had just five days from the end of his business accounting period to the end of the tax year to calculate his pre-tax profits and make a pension contribution that produced the maximum amount of higher-rate tax relief.

Most business owners would find this difficult if not impossible to do and very few accountants would work to such a tight deadline.

Some business owners have a 5th of April year end and therefore no time at all to accurately calculate their pre-tax profits.

Uncertainty about the level of pre-tax profits is less of a problem for business owners who are confident their profits will significantly exceed the higher-rate threshold, especially if their pension contributions are quite modest (for example, someone who reckons pre-tax profits will be £80,000 and wants to make an £8,000 pension contribution).

Uncertainty about the level of pre-tax profits could be a problem for high earners who are making big catch-up pension contributions and want higher-rate tax relief on the whole amount (for example, someone who expects roughly £90,000 of pre-tax profit and wants to make a £40,000 pension contribution).

Changing the Accounting Year End

One way to overcome this problem has been to change the accounting year end to a date other than the tax year. Let's say the business year end is 30th April 2022. This date falls into the 2022/23 tax year which means the business owner has from 30th April 2022 until the end of the tax year on 5th April 2023 to draw up accounts and decide what pension contribution to make.

Unfortunately it won't be possible to employ this strategy much longer. The Government is proposing that from 2024/25 onwards self-employed people must be taxed on a *tax year basis*. More information about these changes and tax planning opportunities is contained in the Taxcafe guide *Small Business Tax Saving Tactics*.

(Note, if your business currently has a 31st March year end it will be able to keep this date for tax purposes because this is viewed as close enough to the end of the tax year.)

As a result of these changes many self-employed individuals will find it more difficult in future to work out their relevant UK earnings for pension contributions. Those serious about maximising the tax relief on their contributions may have to make an estimate of their profits before the end of the tax year.

The introduction of Making Tax Digital on 6th April 2024 may make this less challenging. Under MTD the self employed will have to submit quarterly reports of their income and expenses anyway.

Chapter 36

Pension Planning for Property Investors

When I started out writing this guide, I planned to conduct a comprehensive study comparing pensions and buy-to-let property. However, I quickly abandoned this idea for two reasons.

Firstly, a pension is not an asset, it's simply a 'wrapper' that protects the underlying assets from tax. Those assets are normally shares and bonds and sometimes commercial property (but not residential property which is prohibited).

So any comparison between pensions and buy-to-let ultimately boils down to a comparison between stock market investing and residential property investing.

Plenty of academics have conducted studies to see which asset class performs best but the results are sensitive to the time period under consideration and, critically, whether you include rents and dividends in the analysis.

The second reason why I decided not to spend time comparing pensions and buy-to-let property is that many property investors would simply not countenance investing in anything else. "Nothing beats bricks and mortar," goes the popular mantra.

I've lost count of the number of times I've heard the phrase "my properties are my pension".

So what I've decided to do in this chapter is explore whether a pension can be used to *complement* an investment in buy-to-let property.

This is particularly important now that tax relief on mortgage interest has been reduced.

Many landlords have seen their tax bills rise significantly but it may be possible to mitigate the effects by making pension contributions.

Changes to Mortgage Tax Relief

Tax relief for interest and finance costs paid by individual landlords who own residential properties is now restricted.

Higher-rate tax relief has been replaced with tax relief at the 20% basic rate.

The new rules do not apply to commercial properties or furnished holiday lettings or to properties held inside companies.

The reduced tax relief on mortgage interest means many landlords now have significantly bigger *taxable* rental profits, even if their true rental profits remain unchanged.

Using Pensions to Beat the Tax Increase

A simple way for landlords to beat the tax increase is by making pension contributions.

How much will you need to invest to claw back all the extra tax you'll pay? As a rule of thumb, your *gross* pension contribution will need to be half as big as your mortgage interest.

So if you have £10,000 of buy-to-let interest you will typically need to make a gross pension contribution of £5,000 to recover the extra tax you will pay.

Example – Before Pension Contribution

Usman earns £60,000 as a self-employed consultant and a rental profit of £10,000 (after deducting £10,000 of buy-to-let interest) from residential property.

If Usman's mortgage tax relief was NOT restricted he would have total taxable income of £70,000 and his total after-tax income this year would be:

£70,000 income - £15,432 income tax = £54,568

However, with his mortgage interest no longer tax deductible, Usman's income tax bill increases by £2,000 to £17,432 (he will have an extra £10,000 of rental income taxed at 40% but will also be entitled to a tax reduction equal to 20% of his mortgage interest).

In summary, his after-tax income will fall from £54,568 to £52,568.

(Usman's national insurance has been ignored for simplicity.)

Example – After Pension Contribution
Usman decides to invest £4,000 in his pension. The taxman will add £1,000 of basic-rate tax relief, giving him a gross pension contribution of £5,000.

He will also receive higher-rate tax relief through his self-assessment tax computation. This is calculated as 20% of his gross pension contribution: £5,000 x 20% = £1,000.

In total Usman enjoys £2,000 tax relief by making a £5,000 gross pension contribution (a cash contribution of £4,000). Hence, all the extra tax arising due to the reduction in his interest relief is clawed back by making a gross pension contribution half as big as his mortgage interest payments.

Pensions: Cashflow Issues

Although you can completely reverse the tax increase by making pension contributions, there is one significant problem: your money is locked away until you reach the minimum retirement age (currently 55).

In other words, pension contributions can seriously damage your cashflow!

We saw that Usman's disposable income falls from £54,568 to £52,568 with his mortgage tax relief restricted.

By making a pension contribution he claws back £2,000 and ends up with £54,568 again BUT £5,000 of that is stuck inside a pension plan!

His actual disposable income will fall by a further £3,000 to £49,568. Usman's financial position is summarised below:

Usman: Tax Relief versus Cash Flow

	No Pension Contribution	Pension Contribution
	£	£
Sole trader profit	60,000	60,000
Taxable rental profit	20,000	20,000
	---------	---------
	80,000	80,000
Less:		
Income tax	17,432[1]	16,432[2]
Pension contribution	0	4,000
Mortgage interest[3]	10,000	10,000
Disposable income[4]	**52,568**	**49,568**
Pension Pot	**0**	**5,000**

Notes
1. First £12,570 tax free, next £37,700 taxed at 20%, final £29,730 taxed at 40%. Reduced by £2,000 tax reduction (mortgage interest x 20%).
2. Further reduced by £1,000 higher-rate tax relief on pension contribution.
3. Taxable rental profit is not the same as actual rental profit; his £10,000 of mortgage interest must be deducted to calculate his true disposable income.
4. Ignores national insurance payments. These would be the same under both scenarios and hence do not alter the overall conclusion.

Why does Usman's disposable income fall by £3,000? Because he personally invests £4,000 into his pension but gets £1,000 of higher-rate tax relief back when he submits his tax return.

In summary, for every £10,000 of mortgage interest you pay, you will generally be able to claw back the extra tax you face as a higher-rate taxpayer by making a £5,000 gross pension contribution.

£3,000 will come from you and £2,000 from the taxman. Thus, your disposable income will also fall by £3,000.

238

Protecting Your Child Benefit

So far we've looked at the "bread and butter" case where the landlord is a regular higher-rate taxpayer and enjoys 40% tax relief on the pension contributions. Some landlords may be able to enjoy even more tax relief.

Take a taxpayer whose taxable income has risen from £50,000 (before the tax change) to £60,000 now.

With income over £50,000 he will pay the child benefit charge if he is a parent and the highest earner in his household. In this case a pension contribution will reduce his "adjusted net income" which will also reduce the child benefit charge.

For example, a £5,000 gross pension contribution will reduce his adjusted net income from £60,000 to £55,000 which means his child benefit charge will be halved from £2,636 to £1,318 (if he has three children). In total, Usman will enjoy £3,318 tax relief on his £5,000 pension contribution, i.e. 66% tax relief.

Other Important Tax Thresholds

If your taxable income is pushed over the £100,000 threshold you will start losing your personal allowance. Once your income reaches £125,140 your personal allowance is completely withdrawn this year.

But making pension contributions reduces your adjusted net income which claws back some of your personal allowance. As a result, making pension contributions while your income is in the £100,000-£125,140 tax bracket will generally provide you with 60% tax relief.

If your taxable income gets pushed over the £150,000 tax threshold you will start paying additional rate tax at 45%. The flipside is you can enjoy up to 45% tax relief on any pension contributions you make. From next year (2023/24) onwards additional-rate tax will be payable when your income exceeds £125,140.

Your annual allowance (the maximum amount that can be invested in your pension) may be reduced if your "adjusted income" exceeds £240,000 – See Chapter 20 for more information.

Do You Have Earnings?

Everyone under 75 can make a gross pension contribution of up to £3,600 per year.

If you want to contribute more than this and receive tax relief your gross contributions must not exceed your annual earnings.

Salaries and trading profits are earnings for this purpose; rental profits generally are not. If a landlord wants to make big pension contributions he must have earnings from other sources.

Tax on Withdrawals

Apart from your 25% tax-free lump sum, withdrawals from your pension pot will be fully taxed.

Ultimately, therefore, pension contributions cannot completely reverse the increase in your income tax bill caused by the restriction to mortgage tax relief.

However, with proper timing, you may be able to minimise the tax on your withdrawals and make sure that some of them are tax free or taxed at no more than the 20% basic rate.

Chapter 37

Putting Property into a Pension

Some business owners use a specialist SIPP or other pension plan to hold their business premises and in this chapter we'll take a look at the benefits and drawbacks.

Note that you can put *commercial property* into a pension but not residential property, so this option is not available to buy-to-let landlords.

Holding business property in a pension has a number of benefits:

- **Tax-free rent**. There is no income tax payable by you on the rent your business pays into your pension plan. These rent payments are also a tax deductible expense for the business.

- **No capital gains tax**. When a property held inside a pension is sold there is no capital gains tax payable.

- **Inheritance tax exemption**. Assets held in a pension fall outside your estate for inheritance tax purposes.

Although the ability to roll up rental income tax free inside a pension is enticing, you must never lose sight of the fact that all the money you eventually withdraw from your pension, over and above your 25% tax-free lump sum, will be subject to income tax.

If you are a higher-rate taxpayer at present but expect to be a basic-rate taxpayer when you retire, it's possible the rental income will ultimately be much less heavily taxed by going the pension route.

Similarly, although property held inside a pension can be sold without incurring capital gains tax, when you eventually withdraw the capital gain most of it (75%) will be subject to income tax.

If you are a basic-rate taxpayer when you retire you will currently pay 20% tax and if you are a higher-rate taxpayer you will pay 40% tax.

By contrast, if you sell commercial property that you own personally you will be subject to capital gains tax. Commercial property benefits from the lower 20% CGT rate and it's possible some of the gain will be taxed at just 10% if your basic-rate band isn't used up by your other income.

In some cases a sale of business premises owned personally will qualify for Business Asset Disposal Relief. If so, a tax rate of 10% may apply to the whole gain, although the relief will be restricted if your company has paid you rent at any time since 6th April 2008.

Business premises held inside your pension do not have to be sold when you retire. If your own business ceases to occupy the property, the property can remain in your pension and be rented out to someone else and the rent will roll up tax free in your pension.

Although property held inside your pension may fall outside your estate for inheritance tax purposes, in most cases the family members that inherit your pension pot will have to pay income tax on any money they subsequently withdraw.

By contrast, if you own your business premises personally, the property may qualify for business property relief (100% inheritance tax exemption if you are a sole trader, 50% if the business is used by your partnership or company).

Finally, when it comes to tucking away money inside a pension we must never lose sight of the fact that you will not be able to get your hands on any of the money until you are at least 55 (rising to 57 in 2028).

Clearly there are benefits to holding business property inside a pension but it is by no means a 'no brainer'. There are benefits but also drawbacks and each case would have to be decided on its merits with help from a professional.

Funding the Property Purchase

The purchase of a business property by a pension can be funded in several ways. Typically you will use your existing pension savings, topped up with fresh contributions (including company pension contributions if you run a company).

It is also possible for your pension fund to borrow money but only up to 50% of its net assets. For example, if you have pension savings of £100,000 an additional £50,000 can be borrowed.

Some pension providers allow a part share in a property to be acquired by the pension plan, with the balance owned outside the pension.

Several individuals can also pool their pension savings to collectively buy a property.

Transferring Existing Property

If you already own the property you can sell it to your SIPP and this may allow you to release a sizeable amount of cash from your pension savings.

Transferring an existing property into a pension is likely to result in capital gains tax becoming payable if the property has risen in value since you bought it.

Commercial property benefits from the lower 20% CGT rate and some of the gain may be taxed at just 10% and some may be tax-free thanks to the annual CGT exemption although, this is being drastically reduced over the next couple of years. It is unlikely Business Asset Disposal Relief would be available in such cases.

A sizeable capital gains tax bill may put off many existing property owners going down the pension route but others may still be tempted by the prospect of receiving a large cash payment out of their pension savings.

The transfer may also result in a stamp duty land tax bill and VAT may also be payable in certain circumstances, although a VAT refund can usually be claimed.

In Specie Contributions

Properties have also been transferred into pensions as *in specie* pension contributions, with the member claiming income tax relief. *In theory* a property worth, say, £100,000 would be transferred into the pension scheme with the scheme administrator claiming £25,000 of basic-rate tax relief to add to the member's pension pot and the member themselves claiming higher-rate tax relief when they submit their tax return.

In specie contributions are no longer permitted by most pension firms following a clamp down by HMRC because of perceived abuse. In a recent case, the Upper Tribunal ruled that tax relief was not available on an in specie contribution of shares and some in the pensions industry fear HMRC may now attempt to reclaim millions of pounds of tax relief on past in-specie contributions.

Costs and other Formalities

Not all pension providers deal with property purchases so you may need to transfer your existing pension savings to a specialist provider.

When your property is held inside a pension your business will have to be treated just like any other tenant, with no special favours, which means rent will have to be paid at a full market rate come hell or high water.

If rent is not paid this will be treated as an unauthorised payment by your pension and HMRC may levy a charge of 40% on you personally and a charge of up to 40% on the pension itself.

Property SIPPs are also much more expensive to run than those that only allow you to invest in traditional 'stocks and shares'.

Initial set up costs include legal fees, surveyor fees, lenders fees and fees to the pension company managing your SIPP.

Fees will have to be paid for regular rent revaluations and a third party property manager may have to be appointed to collect the rent from you.

Part 9

Family Pension Planning

Chapter 38

Couples: Who Should Make the Pension Contributions?

People who don't have any earnings (i.e. who don't work) can still make a small pension contribution and receive tax relief.

The current limit is £3,600 per year with £2,880 per year coming from the individual and £720 from the taxman in basic-rate tax relief.

Is this worth doing?

Some people think it is because, although there will only be basic-rate tax relief, the ultimate pension income may end up being completely tax free, covered by the individual's income tax personal allowance.

The broader question that needs answering is this:

Under what circumstances should you transfer money to your spouse or partner to make pension contributions?

We will try to answer this question with the aid of a case study.

Case Study

Rory is a higher-rate taxpayer and his wife Claire is either a basic-rate taxpayer or doesn't work at all (whichever you prefer). Rory contributes to a pension, Claire doesn't. The couple want to make an additional small pension contribution (for Claire this cannot exceed £3,600) and are trying to decide *who* should make it.

Rory will enjoy higher-rate tax relief if he makes the contribution BUT he expects to ultimately pay income tax at the basic rate on his pension income. Claire will only enjoy basic-rate tax relief if she makes the contribution BUT she hopes to pay 0% tax on her pension income (thanks to her income tax personal allowance).

Let's assume the couple want to save an additional £1,000. If Claire makes the contribution the taxman will add £250 of basic-rate tax relief, producing a gross pension contribution of £1,250.

Rory can make a net cash contribution of £1,333. The taxman will add £333 of basic-rate relief, resulting in a gross contribution of £1,666. Rory will also receive £333 of higher-rate tax relief (£1,666 x 20%), so the net cost to him is also £1,000 (£1,333 cash contribution - £333 higher-rate relief).

Rory has an extra £1,666 going into his pension, whereas Claire only has £1,250.

Rory's pension contribution is 33% bigger than Claire's.

Withdrawing Income

How much money will Claire or Rory have when they ultimately withdraw this money from their pensions and pay any income tax due?

We can ignore any investment growth on their contributions as it doesn't affect the overall outcome. We will also ignore any future contributions to keep the example simple.

They can both take a 25% tax-free lump sum. The remaining 75% will be taxed when withdrawn.

Their positions are summarised in Table 7. The total after tax includes the tax-free lump sum and the income remaining after paying income tax at either 0%, 20% or 40%.

For example, if Rory's gross contribution is £1,666 he will be able to take a tax-free lump sum of £416. If the remaining £1,250 is taxed at 20% he will be left with £1,416 in total after tax.

The example is simplistic but does offer some interesting insights.

Table 7
Couples Pension Planning
Who Should Make Contributions?

	Higher-rate relief on contributions	Basic-rate relief on contributions
	£	£
"Pension pot"	1,666	1,250
25% Tax-free	416	312
75% Taxable	1,250	938
Total after tax:		
After-tax @ 0%	1,666	1,250
After-tax @ 20%	1,416	1,062
After-tax @ 40%	1,166	875

When Rory Should Make the Contributions

If Rory pays 20% income tax when he retires (remember he has other pension savings so this isn't guaranteed) he will end up with £1,416 eventually. If Claire pays 0% income tax (because she has no other pension savings and her pension withdrawals are covered by her income tax personal allowance) she will end up with £1,250. Rory ends up with 13% more money.

So the first conclusion is this: Rory should keep on making the pension contributions, even if Claire's pension income will be tax free.

It may be even more important that Rory makes the contributions if there is any likelihood that Claire will acquire another source of income (e.g. from rental properties, inherited assets, a business or job etc). If Claire ends up being taxed at 20% on her pension income she may end up with £1,062 to Rory's £1,416. Rory ends up with 33% more money in this scenario.

When Claire Should Make the Contributions

But what if Rory, like Claire, does not receive higher-rate tax relief on his additional pension contribution, only basic-rate tax relief? This would be the case if his existing pension contributions are already equal to the amount of income he has taxed at 40% (see Chapter 4 for an explanation).

In this case Rory would end up with £1,062 to Claire's £1,250. Claire receives 18% more income in this scenario.

So the second conclusion is this: Claire should make the additional contributions if Rory cannot obtain any additional higher-rate tax relief and she expects to pay no tax on her pension income. It's a second-best outcome but may be the best route for some couples.

If Rory expects to be a higher-rate taxpayer when he retires (if he has a lot of other pension savings or taxable income) he could end up with £1,166. Claire will end up with £1,250 but only if she pays no tax on her pension withdrawals. If she pays 20% tax she will end up worse off than Rory, even though he pays 40% tax.

In most cases Claire only ends up better off than Rory if she pays 0% tax on her pension income. However, if she works she will eventually receive a taxable state pension which will probably use up a significant chunk of her personal allowance which means she could pay 20% tax on some of her other pension income.

Even if Claire has never worked she may receive some state pension. For example, she will build up state pension entitlement while she has children under 12 and qualifies for child benefit.

In these cases Claire may only be able to pay 0% tax on all her pension income if all her pension savings are withdrawn before she reaches state pension age. This may only be possible if she has a relatively small pension pot.

Less Common Scenarios

There are other permutations, including Rory paying 0% tax when he retires (the best-case scenario of all) and Claire paying 40% tax when she retires (the worst-case scenario of all) but these outcomes are less likely and will not be discussed further.

Avoiding the Child Benefit Charge

If Claire receives child benefit and Rory's adjusted net income is still in the £50,270-£60,000 bracket, he should probably be the one making all the pension contributions (see Chapter 19).

This will allow him to reduce or avoid the child benefit tax charge and enjoy over 50% tax relief on his pension contributions (see Chapter 19).

Family Tax Planning and Other Issues

Finally, it's worth pointing out that Claire may have *non-tax* reasons for making pension contributions, for example if she feels this gives her greater financial security.

On this note it should be pointed out that there are other things the couple can do to make use of Claire's tax-free personal allowance before she receives any state pension. For example, rental properties and other assets could be placed in her name, as could money the couple may eventually inherit.

Lifetime ISAs

These are discussed in detail in Part 3. Those under 40 can save up to £4,000 per year in a Lifetime ISA with a £1,000 Government bonus.

If Claire is under 40 she may prefer to put her money into a Lifetime ISA instead of a pension because the upfront tax relief is currently the same as a pension BUT all her withdrawals will be completely tax free.

Similarly, if Rory expects to be a higher-rate taxpayer when he retires he may be better off investing his additional savings in a Lifetime ISA.

Chapter 39

Pensions for Children and Grandchildren

"When I was a boy of 14, my father was so ignorant I could hardly stand to have the old man around. But when I got to be 21, I was astonished at how much the old man had learned in seven years."
Mark Twain

Everyone under the age of 75 can make a pension contribution of £3,600 per year and receive basic-rate tax relief (which currently reduces the net cost to £2,880).

This means minor children can benefit from pension contributions made by their parents or grandparents.

Many pension providers have special pension plans for minors, like the Junior SIPP from Hargreaves Lansdown. According to HMRC, around 60,000 children under 18 years of age are benefiting this tax break.

Making pension contributions on behalf of a minor child could be a wonderful way to leave an asset of lasting value that cannot be frittered away, at least not until the child is a responsible adult!

These contributions have the added bonus of usually being exempt from inheritance tax, being covered by either the £3,000 annual exemption or the regular gifts out of income exemption.

A pension contribution made on behalf of a minor child could grow into a significant nest egg. For example, let's say you make 18 annual contributions of £2,880 starting in the year a child is born. Each contribution will be topped up with £720 of basic-rate tax relief (even though the child doesn't pay any income tax), producing a gross pension contribution of £3,600 per year.

If we assume that the investments in the pension grow by 7% per year, just before the child's 18th birthday, when the last contribution is made, the pension pot will be worth £122,397. However, that's not the end of the story. The money will continue to compound tax free until the child reaches the minimum retirement age. For example, when the child is 58 the pension pot could be worth close to £2 million.

Of course these figures aren't adjusted for inflation. If some inflation adjustments are made they could still end up with a pension pot worth several hundred thousand pounds in today's money, which is still a tidy sum.

We don't know what the minimum retirement age will be many decades from now – it could be a lot higher than 58 – and that is perhaps one major drawback of contributing to a pension so early.

Junior ISAs

Just like normal ISAs, money grows tax free but there is no upfront tax relief, as there is with pension contributions.

The annual investment limit is currently £9,000.

Unlike regular ISAs, money cannot be withdrawn until the child reaches age 18. From that date the junior ISA becomes an adult ISA and the child can do what he or she likes with the money.

Junior SIPP vs Junior ISA

There's no doubt most children or grandchildren would prefer you to contribute to a junior ISA instead of a junior SIPP. They will face big financial commitments between the age of 18 and retirement age: university fees, mortgages, childcare costs etc.

However, there is a risk that the child will fritter away all of that carefully saved money if they can access it at the tender age of 18.

Personally I prefer the pension route for the simple reason that your children or grandchildren will have to save for retirement anyway. In other words, they can never lose out with a pension but they can lose out with a junior ISA that is not spent wisely.

They'll thank you for it... one day.

Lightning Source UK Ltd.
Milton Keynes UK
UKHW020653180123
415553UK00007B/597